IT'S NEVER

DULL

by Debbe Magnusen

IT'S NEVER DULL!!!

Adventures in the world of adoption/foster care and rescuing babies from abandonment

By
Debbe A. Magnusen

Illustrations
by
Ferd Johnson

IT'S NEVER DULL!

Copyright 1998 by Debbe Magnusen

Published by DeDay Publishing

For information or to
contact Debbe write to: Project Cuddle
2973 Harbor Blvd.#326
Costa Mesa, CA 92626-3989

Designer: Elizabeth W. Richards

Library of Congress Catalog Card Number: 98-96099

ISBN 0-9664196-0-X
1. Title   2. Adoption/Foster   3. Family/Childcare   4. Biography

Printed by: Golden Belt Printing, Inc.
Great Bend, Kansas

NOTE: Some of the stories in this book have had names, locations, dates and identifying characteristics changed in order to protect the privacy and safety of the people involved.

FOREWORD

When Debbe Magnusen asked me to read her new book, <u>It's Never Dull!</u>, and explained that it was a book about abandoned and abused children, it wasn't hard for me to come up with a list of other things I'd rather do. But knowing the author as I do, and experiencing first-hand how deep her passion runs, I started reading and didn't stop until my emotions had run the gamut. I had a new-found respect and admiration for Debbe and her family, as well as for the foster parents and the innocent babies for whom they care.

If you or anyone you know is even remotely concerned when they hear about another child being abused or perhaps abandoned...This book is a must. You'll never find a book which encompasses not only the special problems of drug-exposed and abused children, but also offers an inside view of the frustration and now successes of preventing babies from being abandoned or murdered at birth by their own mothers. However, the constant theme that appears throughout the book is LOVE!

We've all heard the stories about the "foster parents" that were bringing children into their homes for the extra government check...well, you won't find any such stories in this book. In, <u>It's Never Dull!</u>, Debbe Magnusen includes story after story of her personal, and other foster parents', experiences deep in the trenches, fighting for the life and security of their foster kids. This book establishes a reality so strong and clear that anybody thinking about becoming a foster parent for the wrong reasons would be scared off after the first chapter. It also helps us in understanding the fear that women go through when contemplating abandoning their babies.

Obviously any mother willing to continue her drug use during her pregnancy, isn't going to make much of a mother or provider. Neither is a father who dangles his child out the window of a four story apartment because he's angry with the child. Someone must step in and make sure these special children are loved and cared for. Sometimes a foster parent is asked to step in for the duration while a drug-addicted mother completes a re-hab program; and in some cases "the duration" is much longer.

Debbe Magnusen and her husband Dave have two wonderful biological children of their own; and they have adopted five other children who have become permanent members of their family. As a family, they have cared for more than 30 drug-exposed or abused children since 1984. I say "as a family," because caring for one of these special babies takes a unique coordination of a family's attention, unselfish care and most importantly, their love. Debbe and her family are very special people, as are all the people you will encounter in this book.

If you, like me, watch the evening news and are overwhelmed by man's ability to be cruel, dishonest, selfish, etc., etc., then read It's Never Dull!. You'll have an uplifting, joyful, enlightening experience that will move you, and allow you to once again feel mankind's ability to reach out and love and care for his own. You will be left with a feeling of wanting or needing to reach out and help someone. Do it now, you're needed. We love you.

Ted McGinley

DEDICATION

This is dedicated to my wonderful family. I need to thank everyone from my wonderful husband Dave, my parents, Dr. & Mrs. Pyle(Dick & Scotty) and my in-laws, Betty and Bob Gage; and in loving memory of Donald Magnusen, my father-in-law. Your support, encouragement and sense of humor helped in shaping my goals and dreams. I appreciate your standing back in silence as I stumbled my way through the past few years. To Graham and Vernelle Kerr, for believing in me and what I am trying to accomplish. You have no idea how much your friendship means to me and my entire family. To the late Suzanne Haig, for teaching me the art of expressing myself through word and song. This is also dedicated to all "My Babies," past, present and future. I pray God's hand will gently protect you, one and all. Finally, to all those frightened girls and women who took a chance and contacted Project Cuddle and chose not to abandon their babies but instead give their child a chance at life. You can now hold your head high.

THESE DRAWINGS ARE DEDICATED TO DEBBE MAGNUSEN, WHO MAKES GOOD THINGS HAPPEN... FERD JOHNSON

TABLE OF CONTENTS

INTRODUCTION

Life can truly be an adventure, if only we take the time to live it. I can honestly say that my life has been a combination between Mr. Toad's Wild Ride and the female counterpart to Forest Gump. Oh yes, you are going to run into negative situations and people on the journey of life, but the important thing is to go past them and beyond them. Though my greatest desire as a child was to grow up and try to save babies from abandonment, it would take fostering drug-exposed babies and working with their mothers in order to come up with a solution.

Little did I know that some of those negative experiences I had lived through over twenty years ago would have such an impact on what I do today. It's amazing to realize that coming close to death while pregnant with my daughter, Lani, helped me in understanding women who cannot accept their pregnancies. Working with women who have given birth to drug-exposed babies has opened my eyes to things I never knew existed. I don't judge them, and for this reason alone, I know that this was part of an education I would need in order to fulfill the "ultimate" assignment God put me here to accomplish. Now, I save babies. No, not just a baby, but babies that were originally destined for dumpsters in back alleys or even death. Until now, society has looked the other way. Look at almost any town or city in America today and you will find that they have at least once encountered the devastation of having a tiny newborn placed somewhere within their city limits. Some suffer for hours, many for days.

The good news is that now, there is no longer a reason to ask ourselves, "Why don't they leave these abandoned babies at my door step?" Now, with Project Cuddle's 24 hour crisis hot-line in place, frightened, pregnant teens,or women have a place to call; we are a seeing that there are alternatives to this tragic yet all to often ending. At the time of this writing, it has only been 18 months since the creation of Project Cuddle's program and we have already saved 51 babies from such a fate. Now, they have eyes that will see a sunrise and a sunset... ears that will hear the roar of a crowd, as the home team makes the winning touchdown..., legs that feel the joy of being able to run after a ball, and yes even the experience of skinning a knee. Yet this time they will feel the warm embrace of a mother's arms as she comforts and cleans the wound. Ultimately, she will place that magical kiss upon that "boo-boo" and all the pain will magically go away.

This effort is growing nation wide. It's exciting, and also frightening. Exciting because we need volunteers across the country in

9

order to continue saving babies. Frightening, because we will need funds to keep the program in place. For some, it's the thrill of getting your hands dirty that is important, and we look forward to such help. To others, there just isn't enough time in the day to volunteer, even though they care. Trust me when I say, that without dollars continually being donated to charities such as Project Cuddle, Inc. we can't continue efforts to save lives. Every dollar is appreciated. I know that it took me many thousands of dollars when starting up Project Cuddle, Inc. but I felt to guilty to ask for donations. Now, I see that without those continued funds coming in, we won't be able to continue to save precious little babies from the fate of a dumpster or even death.

Hugs and Cuddles,

Dette A. Magnussen

Debbe Magnusen has been working with drug-exposed newborns since 1984. She and her husband, Dave, have cared for over 30 foster children during this time. Eventually, Debbe and her husband adopted five of these wonderful children, so that they now have a total of seven children in the family. But, Debbe's heart has always desired to help protect those who were abandoned at birth. Since she was a little girl she dreamed of helping those tiny victims, yet they were not the children that were brought to her door. Now, with the support from Project Cuddle's Board of Directors, Debbe has developed the first known nation-wide, 24 hour crisis hot-line for girls and women who are contemplating abandoning their babies. By the time you read this, the number of babies saved will probably be much higher than the 51 babies in 18 months that she has currently saved.

The charity that she founded, Project Cuddle, Inc. is now mainly focused on these efforts and is solely funded by individuals who make donations. She has been extremely busy appearing on shows such as 48 Hours, CNN, Extra and many guest appearances on the Geraldo Show where she has reached hundreds of girls. The BBC is working on a documentary for England as well. This past few years the country has begun to take note of the rising crisis of abandoned babies as well as Debbe's efforts to stop this problem. She was recently honored with the prestigious George Washington Medal of Honor from the American Freedom Foundation, as well as an award from CBS entitled, "What's Right with Southern California". Besides being a wife and mother to her seven children, her main goal now is to make the public aware of the fact that there is someone out there who cares, and no desperate, frightened woman or teen needs to abandon her baby. By calling 1-88 TO CUDDLE, OR 1-888-628-3353 They can get CONFIDENTIAL, safe help, thus preventing them from breaking the law, as well as protecting the life of a child, and in many cases creating a new family in the process.

ACKNOWLEDGMENTS

Bushels full of thanks must go to Liz Richards for her talent and time in helping to edit and to furnish production art for this book. The encouragement she gave to me throughout this tedious endeavor is truly appreciated.

A big kiss towards Heaven to "Grandpa Ferdie," AKA Ferd Johnson of the Moon Mullins comic strip for over 65 years. Ferd took my crazy ideas and creatively stroked them into realities. I feel honored that you became a part of my book.

A big, big thanks to Elizabeth Barton! Without your honest input, I doubt that "It's Never Dull!!!" would have ever become something worth reading. Your advice was greatly appreciated. To my dear friends, Yvette Taylor, Valerie O'Brien, Pilar Gil, Kathy Stefano, Wendy Tividad, Rosa Muro-Clark, Kalei Damon, Jon & Pam Blair, Carin Howard and Gloria R. ...THANKS!

To Julia Tischler, who is not only the most beautiful and intelligent attorney I know, but is also honest and sensitive. I know that there is no way that I could have helped in saving all those little babies lives without your expertise and willingness to believe in me, and then help. Thanks Jewels!

To the Divine Bette Midler, the Wonderful Bonnie Bruckheimer and the Adorable Gina Veltri...I love you all and thank you so much for your support.

Dear Shirley Yankie, Kelly Klaus, Saundra Buckley, Heidi Drew, Deanna Maurer, Kathy Simons, Emily McGinley, Kia & Georgia Sexton, thanks for helping so much with the phones, Mary Hibbard and Karlene Gentley, Sheli Hinds...you are jewels. To my second cousin, Nancy Miller and your family, I truly am so glad that I finally got to meet you after our phone interview for this book. I truly admire your strength and the courage that you have shown in carrying on after your husband's death. To my sister Susan for joining our team and my sister Marci who hopes to join us as soon as the funds allow. We sure can use the help!

This book could never have happened if it hadn't been for the patience, love and support shown by my family. Dave, you allowed me to proceed with my crazy hair-brained schemes when you weren't even sure what they were all about. I hope that I can make you proud of what is being accomplished. Lani and Brian, I thank you for putting up with my writing and endless hours at the computer. Those occasions when I paid you a dollar to change a messy diaper will always be appreciated. Bejay, Beth, and Emily, Tyler and Jonathon, I thank you for allowing me to hold you on my lap while I typed and for the privilege of sharing how great you all are in our eyes. I pray that your stories will help in making others aware of how far the abused, abandoned and neglected children of this country can go.

Thanks to all the tiny ones and their mothers that have touched my life and added spice to it's contents. Without you there would be no story.

Hugs and Cuddles,

Debbe

12

Adopt A Teenager?

"Push, honey, push!" I cheered. "You can do it!" Connie and Bob chimed in.

The couple stood side by side, gently leaning against the pane of glass. It was the only thing that separated them from actually being in the delivery room to see the birth of their future child. This couple had tried all the infertility specialists in town, to no avail. They had applied for adoption through this small, private adoption agency over two years before and...finally...their time had come. Now they stood close enough so that they could hear every breath drawn and every pant and puff exhaled in the tiny hospital's only delivery room.

Terry had promised me that she would not deliver her baby on "Jesus' Birthday." Furthermore, she had also promised that she would open her Christmas stocking and gifts with a flat belly.

Here it was, the day before Christmas, and this little fourteen-year old was keeping her promise. Bless her heart, she had even taken castor oil, hoping to start the contractions. (I guess some of those old-fashioned remedies for "what ails ye" really work.)

Five hours after taking the castor oil I had received the call: "Mom, it's me, Terry, and...uh...this is it. I'm scared." I told Terry that I was on my way. It was a two-hour drive to the hospital, so I didn't waste any time getting started.

I kept telling myself to be calm. I even pushed the speed control, so I could not possibly get stopped for speeding. I just didn't have time for that. After all, at the ripe old age of twenty-nine, I was about to become a grandmother.

You ask "How?" "Why?" Well...it's like this. We had always talked about becoming foster parents, and finally got the opportunity to do so with Terry. I guess you could say, we fell into it.

Terry was a fourteen-year old who had been sexually abused by her birth father, Robert. Yes, I said her father. She had become pregnant with her own half-sister. By the time she figured out that she was pregnant, it was too late for an abortion.

Terry's father had desperately tried to get Terry to have an abortion. He knew she was six months along, and he also knew that the only thing linking him to having sexually abused Terry would be that baby. He needed to make sure that the evidence did not exist.

Terry decided the only option she had was to give the baby up for adoption at birth. She was afraid of Social Services, because her father had said, "We'll both go to jail if you tell anyone. You had better keep quiet." Terry called a private adoption agency she found in the phone book. She had no intention of telling them the truth about the baby. She planned to tell them her boy friend had gotten her pregnant.

However, when Jane, the counselor, noticed that Terry's story kept changing, and that there were too many inconsistencies, Jane confronted Terry and asked her to explain why she was trying to protect the real father. She told Terry that the baby and the adoptive family deserved to know the truth. Terry's answers took even this trained counselor by surprise.

We had applied at this same little adoption agency at approximately the same time Terry arrived. Imagine our surprise when the call came: "Hello, Debbe...we have a girl for you...if you're interested." "You're kidding! That was so fast." I was so excited. I couldn't believe that, having applied a brief three weeks previously, we were actually going to adopt. "Oh, gosh, I haven't even bought a crib yet, or bottles or diapers..."

At this point the counselor interrupted me with, "You won't need them. She's already past that stage." Having specifically applied for a newborn, I countered: "Well...how old is she, two or three?" "No, ma'am she's fourteen."

"Fourteen! That's older than my own two kids. Why would someone give her away? I don't get it!"

The counselor began to give me all the ugly details. "We know you originally applied to adopt a baby, but you had mentioned the fact that you hoped to be foster parents someday, and we thought maybe you would like to start with Terry. She can never go home again, so you would be acting as mother and father. Please, will you consider it? We promise to contact you in regard to another baby, as soon as the next one becomes available. We really will call you next."

After catching my breath, I told her I would talk it over with my husband and children, and get back to her in the evening.

"We're almost there, folks!" the doctor said, as a nurse leaned towards him with a sterile towel, wiping his sweaty brow. From the amount of perspiration this man produced, no one would have guessed that it was snowing outside. Snowflakes fell silently to the ground, yet inside this tiny little country hospital, lots of heat was being generated by one and all.

Terry had now been in labor for twelve hours. She was getting tired-but she was a survivor! She had many people cheering her on-her "support group" was on duty!

Our main fear had been for the baby. Would he/she be normal? Would this baby have two arms and legs? Could a child conceived in such ugliness turn out to be a beautiful human being? Maybe it would just take love and nourishment, the kind Terry never received as a child, in order for the infant to make it. It wouldn't be much longer, we hoped, until these questions would be answered.

"I see the head, it's crowning!" the doctor exclaimed. "We love you Terry!" the adoptive mother yelled, as Terry bore down. When the contraction ended Terry inhaled a big breath, then called out into the hallway, "I love you guys, too!" Then she returned to her puffing exercise.

"O.K., now, push, Terry."

"I can't. I'm too tired," she sobbed. "I can't." Terry laid back against the crisp, white pillow. "Please don't make me push any more. Oh, Mommy, it hurts!"

This sent her rooting section into high gear. Connie and Bob stepped into the doorway. I walked up right behind them, and we all started telling her how proud we were of her, etc.

"Now, Terry, just one more push should do it." The doctor gave her the incentive to try one more time. It's funny, but I found myself doing sympathetic pushes right along with her.

For three months prior, the doctor had been telling Terry that it was going to be a girl. The adoptive parents had insisted that Terry be the one to pick out the name, and Terry had become accustomed to calling her Tiffany. As the baby was delivered, the doctor said, "It's a boy!" Terry said, in a voice near panic, "Wait...you said it was going to be a girl." Everyone else in the room could plainly see that it was definitely a GIRL. The doctor's sense of humor seemed to add some joyful atmosphere to a beautiful happening-one that could have turned out to be a very somber occasion.

"Just kidding, Terry...you got your girl, and she looks just fine." Terry's coach, Jane-the woman who had counseled Terry through all those rough months of emotional ups and downs, bent over and whispered into Terry's ear, "You did beautifully, sweetheart, and I'm proud of you." Jane then placed a kiss on Terry's right cheek.

The adoptive father, Daddy Bob, and his wife, Mommy Connie, embraced and cried. I kept clicking the camera, trying to catch as much as I could on film. Bob and Connie had decided someday they would share these pictures with their adopted daughter. They wanted her to know that she was an extremely special little girl.

Somehow, the miracle of the birth of a child can never be explained in words-and this is probably because God wants us to hold it in our hearts, with all the emotions we can muster.

The tiny baby had her umbilical cord cut, then took her first breath of air. As she shrieked her first cries for all the world to hear, she was wrapped, then handed to Terry. With tears in her eyes, she looked at her daughter, who was also her half-sister. "Hi there, Tiffany. How are you?" Terry had been practicing what she would say to her baby for the past month. She finally got to talk with this beautiful child, in person. Terry picked up Tiffany's tiny hand and as she did, the baby's grip tightened around the new mother's finger. "Look at that, Mom, she's holding on already. Boy, she's going to be a smart one." Terry beamed from ear to ear, pleased at her accomplishment of bettering herself as well as giving life to her daughter.

"We need to place her in an incubator now, to get her temperature stabilized." The nurse gently scooped the little babe into her arm, carrying her towards the doorway where we now stood. "Would you like to take a peek?" the nurse said, as she pulled the blanket away from Tiffany's face, revealing a beautiful baby with tiny curls softly framing her little face. We all thought she looked a lot like her birth Mommy.

We followed the nurse down the corridor to the newborn nursery. She walked into a small room containing only the basics. There was a large steel sink against the back wall, with a scale resting on the counter top to the right. In front was a rocking chair of oak, with a pressed design on the head rest. The adoptive parents, as well as Jane and I, all crowded around the doorway, trying to watch as Tiffany was weighed and measured. She didn't like either procedure, and made sure everyone knew it.

After the vital statistics were recorded we watched as she was given her first bath, then wrapped tightly in a clean blanket. The nurse handed the baby to the adoptive mother. "Here you go, little Mommy, try giving her this and let's see how she does." She handed Connie a small bottle of glucose and water, which Tiffany took very quickly and drank a full ounce before falling asleep. Just as the nurse was getting ready to place Tiffany back in the incubator, and official from the health department entered the room.

"Excuse me, I'm here to draw blood from...uh...(looking through papers she pulled out one, read it)..."let me see...baby girl Saunders. We are planning to do paternity tests," she coldly stated, waiting anxiously for the nurse to indicate which baby was the one to be tested.

"Oh, she just went to sleep," Connie whispered, hoping this would make the intruder go away. "Can't we wait until she wakes up?" she sweetly asked.

"I'm sorry, ma'am, but that won't be possible. You see, I was sent here from Los Angeles County, and that means I have a four hour drive...if I'm lucky and don't hit too much traffic. I'll have to go ahead now." She turned toward the nurse. "I assume this is the baby in question."

"Yes, she is," the nurse nodded.

"Let's put her over here on the counter top, while I draw the blood," the stern woman commanded. I felt this was my chance to exit. As I started to walk out of the room, I could see Terry being rolled out of the operating room. Just as we started to pass the nursery, we heard Tiffany's blood-curdling screams, as she experienced her first pain in this cruel world.

Terry had been lying back, rather peacefully taking in the whole feeling of this chapter in her life coming to a close. When she heard Tiffany's screams, she perked up, glancing toward the nursery door. "What's the matter with her? Why is she screaming like that?" I walked along beside the gurney, and was about to tell her the reason, when I saw a look on Terry's face that lead me to believe she had figured out why.

"Mommy, will you stay here for awhile?" she asked in that baby tone I had learned to live with. She still puckered her lips when asking- yes, she still was a little girl, even after all she had just gone through.

Terry fell into a deep sleep, while I sat at the end of the bed. Unfortunately, her sleep had to be interrupted by the specialist with her needle. I held Terry's hand while the procedure started.

This was not like your normal blood test. Everything had to be signed by the person drawing the blood, as well as being witnessed by the nurse in charge. These samples were then placed in a carrying case, which was then locked to guarantee that they were not damaged nor tampered with in transit. Everything had to be very official, but it seemed that the woman in charge could have been just a little more sensitive to Terry's situation. To keep Terry's mind busy, I asked the official if she had to draw blood very often in situations of incest. Much to my surprise, it's something that occurs much more often than I ever thought possible. It is basically a standard procedure for girls who have become pregnant through incest to be aborted. Still, many cases are discovered too late, and must go full term.

I started to realize what a sheltered life I had led. I couldn't believe anything like this could really happen in America, much less in my own community.

Until this point in time I had always worried about and cared for little helpless animals which had no one else to care for them. I now realize how silly I was, putting so much time and attention into God's creatures, when I could have been spending that same effort and emotion on God's children!

When I was only four I had found three abandoned kittens; after caring for them, I knew I would always care for the helpless, in one way or another. Terry's entry into our lives was a rude awakening for us all-but one that was definitely needed. Before Terry officially handed Tiffany over to Bob and Connie, she had requested that we all join together for a word of prayer and dedication for the baby and for the new family of which she was about to become a part. Terry had purchased a special little outfit for this occasion. It was white with pink trimming and smocking across the top. It was way too big, but no one mentioned this, as she awkwardly tried to dress her daughter for the first and yes, the last time. She talked to Tiffany as she pulled one tiny arm into first one big sleeve, then the other.

The pastor from the neighborhood church arrived around three in the afternoon. He stopped in the archway of the door, taking in this beautiful sight. He spoke with Terry, then with Tiffany's new parents; they, as well as Jane and I, joined hands around Terry and her baby, thanking God for His newest creation and praying for God's hand on one and all in the days to come. Afterwards, the pastor dedicated Tiffany while she was held by her new mother. Her new father stood proudly behind the two main ladies of his life. Yes, God had truly been good to them. There wasn't a dry eye in the room when the prayer and dedication were over. After a moment's pause, Terry got up out of the hospital bed. "Well, I guess this is it, Tiffany. You take care of your new Mom and Dad for me." Then she kissed her gently on the forehead, touching one of the many curls framing her baby face.

I picked up Terry's suitcase and followed behind her as she made her way toward the hall. We stopped at the window in the hospital foyer. Outside, life had gone on as usual with one exception: it was still snowing, and excitement over this very unusual weather filled the air. Nurses were scraping together the little bit of snow that hadn't melted, trying to form snowballs to throw at each other. Grownups participated in the joy of this Christmas Eve day, as they probably had when they were just children.

I unlocked the passenger door to let Terry into her side. She moved so slowly. I began to remember what the pain was like after giving birth. I had forgotten all of that, because the joy of having children and watching them grow far outweighed that pain. I wondered if the pain would disappear as easily for Terry. We drove home and Terry quickly fell into a deep and much-needed sleep.

The following morning we celebrated Christ's birth, sharing in a gift exchange at both my husband Dave's and my family's homes. Terry had certainly been true to her word: she opened her gifts on a great big lap and was extremely happy to see something besides maternity clothes in those gift boxes. From what I was seeing, I had a pretty good idea that Terry was going to make it just fine!

Update...

Terry has moved back to the area she originally came from. She decided to try to work things out with her mother, if that was at all possible. She has been gone for over ten years now, but I still think of her often...especially at Christmas.

Her father showed up for the paternity tests, required by the court. The results came back two months later, and they proved that he was definitely the father of Terry's baby.

One thing that hurt Terry more than anything else was the fact that after her father submitted to the blood tests, he skipped the state. She was so angry that she had gone through court testimony for nothing. She had to sit and listen to her father's attorney as he tried to make her feel guilty for what had gone on between her and her father. He made her recount all the sordid details of the "supposed" encounters. Now he was walking free somewhere, while she carried the scars of his selfish desires.

Three years after we heard the results of the blood test, I received a call from the detective on the case. She told me they had finally caught Terry's father in another state, and he was to be transferred to the west coast to stand trial. The father is now serving time in jail, and will not be a free man for many years to come.

The adoption of Tiffany was finalized almost one year after she was placed with Connie and Bob. It had been hard for Terry to take the final step in signing those papers, but she eventually realized that if she loved her daughter enough, she would go ahead and sign off her rights, so that Tiffany could get on with her life. Terry has finished high school since that time, is now a young adult, out on her own. She is working, attending counseling, hoping some day to have a family of her own. "Someday, Mom, I'm going to take my kids to the snow," she had told me as we drove away from that little country hospital, on that cold Christmas Eve.

Bonnie - Our First Drug-Exposed Baby

After our first experience with a teenager, Dave and I agreed that it would be better for all of us if we took in something that was short and compact. Something that would move when I wanted it to.. One thing we realized from working with a child who was older than our own: it caused our eldest, most passive child, Brian, a lot of frustration. His spot in the birth order had been challenged, and he was not at all happy about it.

After letting the county know what type of child we were looking forward to caring for, we ran into a small stumbling block. The workers didn't want to place any child in our home under the age of five-we had a pool and a jacuzzi in our back yard which were not fenced off. Because we lived under the flight pattern of the John Wayne Airport, we were now waiting for the county to buy our home. We knew we were second on the list, so our home would be purchased within the next year. It made no sense for us to put out money for fencing when we knew we would never be reimbursed.

The social workers were able to secure a waiver, so that we could care for children from zero to six months of age, or non-mobile babies.

Finally, about the middle of June, our first call came about an available baby. Many, many social workers called in the next few weeks, trying desperately to place their special child in our home. Some of these workers surely could have been car salesmen/women-they could tell us all kinds of wonderful things about each child. We wouldn't have been surprised had the social worker declared, with a straight face, "Don't worry, he doesn't eat much, never gets into trouble, and did I mention he does windows?..."

Finally in July we received a call that sounded perfect for our needs. I wondered if a simple housewife from California could really make a difference in this little child's life.

When I arrived at the facility where I was supposed to pick up a little girl, I was directed to the ESH (Emergency Shelter Home) office. These were the workers who helped place the children when they were first coming into the system. I was rather nervous, hoping I would do a good job with this little life. I had never promised to give such a full commitment to another person's baby before. As I walked toward the office door, I could hear the two workers discussing the case.

"Hi, can we help you?" the tall, thin blonde woman asked.

"Yes, I think I'm in the right place. I'm here to pick up baby girl Sanchez."

"This is the place, all right," the worker replied. She turned toward the other worker and said, "I'll start filling out the paper work, while you go get the baby." Papers had to be signed by both the worker and myself. One gave permission for medical treatment of the child, and the others were all a blur to me. I quickly finished signing each page and then tucked them into my purse, just as the second worker walked through the door with the baby.

In an ugly, old, orange, yellow and brown afghan, lay a beautiful little girl, weighing only 6 pounds, 2 ounces - but perfectly formed in every way.

The social workers explained to me that this baby was taken away from her mother because she was born exposed to cocaine. This was not the first child to whom the mother had given birth-and it probably wouldn't be her last, either.

"Here you go-she's yours," the second worker said as she handed the baby over to my waiting arms. They gave me a bottle of formula to last until I got her home, and a plastic bag containing all the normal little gifts which a new mother is handed when taking her new baby home from the hospital.

I could hardly wait to get her home. I had waited so long for the paper work and for the finger prints to clear that I really never thought that I actually would get a baby. I quickly picked up my handbag and walked out of the office, beaming from ear to ear.

When I arrived at our house, our seven-year old son, Brian, and our six-year old daughter Lani were there at the front door, waiting to greet our new little guest. Lani was quick to pick up the little bundle and to start asking questions. I decided to set up one rule right then and there: the children were to be allowed to pick up and hold the baby only when I was in the room, and they had to be seated. I was rather nervous at the realization that this was someone else's baby, and I didn't want to take any chances.

"Boy, she's so tiny," Brian said. "How come she's so little?"

"Well, Brian, she was born with drugs in her body. Her mother took them when she was pregnant. The chemicals are still in the baby's body."

"Why would anybody do something like that?" Lani asked, as she played with the tiny fingers on Bonnie's hand and added "You're too pretty and little to have that junk inside you."

"I don't know the answer to that question, honey...I just don't know."

As I unwrapped Bonnie so I could change her diaper, I saw the trembling that we had been trained to look for in a drug-exposed baby. Her clenched fists jerked back and forth uncontrollably. She became

23

very agitated by the fact that her diaper was being changed, and she let out that high-pitched scream to which someday I would become accustomed.

I tightly rewrapped the baby in a crisp, clean blanket that I had been saving for just such an occasion. I swaddle-wrapped her, the way they do in the hospital. It took quite a few minutes to calm her down, but eventually she fell into a deep sleep.

This gave me a moment to get my thoughts together. I started to panic. This was a real drug-exposed baby. What could go wrong? Sure, I wanted to take care of her, but what was I supposed to do for her that was special? I didn't want to "blow it."

I called a woman whose name was on the ESH list. Carol had cared for over ninety babies, almost all "high-risk." It was great having someone who understood what I was going through-someone to reassure me, and to give me a few pointers on Bonnie's care. When I hung up the phone, I felt I would be able to cope after all.

Bonnie remained in our care until the courts decided that custody would go to her grandmother. One day, a call came advising me that I should be prepared to have Bonnie leave within the hour.

We all said our good-byes, then helped load her and her things into our car.

We had given her love and warmth while we had her, and now we prayed God's blessing on her as she traveled on.

Update...

After Bonnie went to live with her grandmother I never heard from the family again. I often wondered what had happened to my first baby. While attending one of the six-month reviews at the Juvenile Court building, I ran into Bonnie and her uncle. It's funny but even though Bonnie was only a little baby when she left, I still recognized her. The uncle was able to tell me that the girl standing by his side was being adopted by her grandmother. She was happy and healthy now, and had a place to call home and a woman to call "Mom."

Marcos

Our next placement came two days later. I wish I could say it was as simple as our first-but I can't.

This time I was told to go to the Intensive Care Unit of our community hospital. There I would find Marcos Martinez, lying in one of the five incubators in the far left-hand corner of the room. I could only make out facial features of three of the babies because of the distance. Two looked average-but the third, who wore a little blue cap on his head, had eyes that seemed to be bulging out of their sockets. I said to myself, "Gee, I hope that's not Marcos." The nurse approached me with the appropriate papers, and after signing them, I was given the funny looking baby with the little blue hat.

He was very awkward to hold. He weighed only five pounds, and 80% of that weight seemed to be located in his head. I carried Marcos out to the car. While driving home, I prayed for guidance with this child. I love a challenge-and this certainly was one!

Everything seemed to be going well until I fed Marcos. He threw everything up. He got me, the carpet, and himself. We all smelled of rotten formula. I called his nurse and asked what his feeding habits had been before I got him. Had he thrown up before? What about his medical records-could I see them, or have access to them? I was told he'd not had any problems, and not to worry. Boy were they wrong!!

That first night I'll never forget. We decided that we couldn't stand the smell that Marcos still had after just being wiped down. He was definitely going to need a full bath.

I went to the kitchen and started the sink water. As the sink filled with luke-warm water, I began to undress this tiny, bug-eyed little boy. I guess the closest resemblance Marcos had to anyone was to the facial structure and features of an "alien". His bald head was shaped like an upside-down pear. His skin was extremely dark, due to medications.

As I undressed him, the long, thin shunt tubing, which lay beneath his skin and ran from the top of his skull, down the side of his neck, ending up in his abdomen looked like an oversized vein. It made me queasy. "Oh, my gosh, what have I gotten into?" I wondered. I had no idea.

As I lowered Marcos into the sink he kicked backward with his feet, thrusting himself backwards. He ended up pushing himself out of my hands and into the sink, now full of water.

"Quick, Dave, get me the bulb syringe!" I yelled, as I turned the baby on his side and tried to drain his mouth as he gasped for air. Dave handed me the syringe and I immediately started suctioning the bath water from his mouth and nose.

"Forget the bath, Dave-I have him breathing again, and I just want him to stay calm, and breathing regularly." I said. I wrapped little Marcos in a soft, blue towel, then held him to my chest. "Thank God he's all right," I sighed. "Boy did that scare me."

I learned in the following days that Marcos had been born three months early, and had never had a regular bath. I probably scared him to death. All he'd ever known was someone trying to weave a wash cloth between the heart monitor lead wires, or using a Q-tip with alcohol around the tubes leading from his bladder to a bag on the side of his incubator.

I diapered him in one of his preemie diapers and put him in a little preemie outfit that would have fit Lani's Cabbage Patch doll. Marcos stayed with us for the next three months. He was able to gain half a pound a week, with the small feedings I continued to give him around the clock.

One evening, I held Marcos in my arms, while my son and I sat watching TV As I held Marcos, I noticed he stiffened up. His eyes rolled around in his head, while Brian and I sat in shock, trying to figure out what was wrong with him.

"Get ready to dial 911 Brian, if I say to." "O.K., Mom," he replied. Marcos finally relaxed, and stopped rolling his eyes around. My guess was that he had some sort of seizure. I was definitely going to have to get in touch with his neurologist.

Eventually, Marcos was placed in the hospital because he had relapsed with the flu. When a baby with a shunt gets dehydrated, it doesn't take long for severe problems to develop. When they got ready to release him, they told me they were not sure if they would be sending him home on a heart monitor or not. I told them, "If he doesn't come home on a monitor, I won't take him." I knew in my heart that this was something he needed.

The night before I was to pick up Marcos, I got a call from the head doctor on call at 10:30 p.m. He told me that Marcos' heart monitor alarm had sounded, and that he had aspirated his formula. They were able to revive him right away, but I would not be able to pick him up, as originally planned.

I went and sat with Marcos for the majority of the day. I asked the nurse why he had aspirated. She said that she wasn't sure. I then asked her how much formula they had been feeding him, and how often. She looked at the charts and said, "Well, it looks like he's been fed between three and four ounces every three to four hours."

"Wait a minute! I told the nurse when we brought him in that he needed one to two ounces every one to two hours. Why weren't they doing this? If you feed him more, he will throw up. That's probably why he aspirated."

"We just don't have the time to feed him that often. There aren't enough of us to take that much time. He'll just have to get used to larger amounts."

I wasn't thrilled with what this woman had just told me. I felt that we were setting Marcos up for more problems. In the morning, I planned to talk with the head doctor. Why had the feedings been increased so rapidly?

At three o'clock in the morning, the doctor called. He said, "I have some bad news for you, Mrs. Magnusen."

I started to brace myself. Was this going to be a call telling me Marcos had died? Please, no. Not that, I thought.

"Marcos had another episode tonight. We have put him into Intensive Care. We aren't sure why he is having problems, but we want to watch him more closely, to get to the bottom of this. I breathed a sigh of relief. "Oh, good. He's alive. I was afraid you were going to tell me he was dead."

"I'm sorry, I didn't mean to scare you. If you would like to come to ICU in the morning, I can explain the procedures we will be doing on Marcos in the next few days. These tests should give us answers to a lot of questions we now have."

I arrived at the hospital next morning, very anxious to see how Marcos was doing. I stopped by the cafeteria to pick up a couple of snacks. I was planning that with them in my purse, I wouldn't have to leave Marcos' side.

I asked for directions to the ICU nurses' station, and told them who I was there to see. My eyes wandered from side to side as I took in all the pathetic little limp bodies occupying both cribs and beds. The nurse pointed to the far back wall and said, "The center bed. His nurse will be there to talk with you in a moment." Each nurse was assigned to either one or two patients. You could tell if your child was considered to be the worst, because that nurse would have only cared for your child alone. Marcos was assigned to a nurse caring for two patients.

She took me over to the side of Marcos' bed. "We had a pretty good night. Today he'll be having a P.H. study done. This will tell us whether or not he has a problem holding his food down or not. If he does, there are medications they may try, in order to keep the problem under control." She turned toward me. "Would you like to hold him?"

"Oh, can I? I mean, he has all those wires and tubes..."

"It's no problem. We can do it. Just have a seat in the rocker right there." She gently lowered Marcos into my waiting arms. "So you're his mother, huh?" "No, I'm his foster mom," I said without looking away from his big, brown eyes.

"Oh, I figured you were his mother, the way you were acting towards him."

"I just try to love them while I have them. Right now Marcos is the one I have, so he gets all the TLC I can muster," I told her.

"I don't think I have seen many foster parents in here before besides you and Leslie Finch."

"I know her-she's had one little girl for quite a long time. That little girl has gone through so much."

"She's down on fourth floor right now. She keeps fighting. You never know-you may see her while Marcos is up here," she told me.

A doctor approached me while I sat rocking Marcos. "Hello there. My name is Dr. Rain. I'll be the doctor doing the P.H. study on Marcos this morning. She had a very pleasant voice. She wore her long, blonde hair in a ponytail. She had a very attractive face, but was conservative with her makeup.

As we talked, the alarm on the baby next to Marcos started going off. The doctor excused herself and promptly went over to assist the frail little boy, who couldn't have been more than eight months old.

Some code was announced over the intercom, and personnel from all departments began arriving, doing what each of them did best to help the child. The mother stood back away from his incubator; holding her hands to her face, she sobbed silently. She knew her son was dying, and there was nothing she could do to help him. In just a few minutes his mouth and fingertips began to turn blue; it certainly didn't look good.

A priest came in to give the baby his last rites. When he finished, we were all asked to leave the area so the medical staff could proceed more quickly. I walked out with the little boy's mother. I asked her if she would like some coffee or tea while we waited for the doctors to get her son's health under control. She said she would take some tea.

As I went over to fix her tea, the social worker in charge of ICU area came over to the woman and escorted her to a private room. I finished fixing the tea, and took it to her. As I left the room, the mother was being told that the doctors didn't feel her son would make it through the next few hours. I began to pray for this poor little boy, and for the mother whose heart was breaking in the adjacent room. Thirty, forty, then fifty minutes went by before we saw the first doctors emerge from the double doors leading to ICU. As one doctor approached, you could see the anguished look on his face. But instead of walking into the room where the mother was sitting, he approached me. I asked myself, "Why is he coming towards me-doesn't he know the mother is in the room over there?"

"Mrs. Magnusen?" he asked in a solemn tone. "I'm Dr. Summers, and I'm helping work with your foster child at the moment."

"What do you mean? I thought Dr. Rain was in charge of Marcos..."

"Yes, she was the one doing the test, but, unfortunately there was a problem, and...well...we lost him for a moment, but we were able to finally revive him."

Thoughts started spinning around in my head. Maybe if I had been there, this wouldn't have happened. Oh, my gosh, we almost lost him. Here I was, praying for this other woman's baby, while mine was in there fighting for his own life, and I didn't even know it.

"Mrs. Magnusen? Mrs. Magnusen?..." Vaguely I heard the doctor, and saw the sympathy in his dark blue eyes. I came back to reality and asked "Is Marcos going to be all right?"

"We don't know. We had to put him on a life support system. He is unable to breathe on his own. It's just going to take time, before we know anything. We called his social worker, and she is on her way over to be with you...I'm sorry," he said as he walked back through the double doors.

As I stood there, not knowing what to do, Leslie-the other foster mother, whose child was down on the fourth floor, came over to me and gave me a hug. "Hi Debbe - is there anything I can do to help? I heard there was a problem with your baby."

I started to cry as she held me in her arms. "I'm so afraid he's going to die."

Leslie and I hadn't known each other very long, but we had some-thing in common-we were both in love with another woman's baby, and both had experienced the long nights, and the pain of watching them suffer. We had both felt that hurt, when the birth mother showed up, when we heard them say, "Come to Mommy." In our hearts, we knew WE were the ones the babies thought was "mom". Where were their mothers now? They had been informed that their children were admitted to the hospital. Why weren't they setting up vigils around the clock? Even though we were only foster parents to these children, we hurt like any real parent would hurt in the same situation.

Barbara from Social Services arrived just then, and told me that she was so sorry this had happened to Marcos. She let me know that they really cared, and that I could reach them at Social Services at any time, if I felt I needed them. Somehow, between the two of them, they decided it would be best if I had someone with me when I saw Marcos for the first time, now that he was on the ventilator.

In my dazed state, I agreed and with Leslie beside me, we slowly walked toward the incubator which still sat at the far back wall of the room. It seemed like an extremely long walk this time. Part of me wanted to get back there in a hurry, but a part of me was very scared. What would I see?

We were within ten feet of his incubator, and we could hear the "woosh, hum" of the ventilator machine. I walked over to his side and could see that his eyes were shut. He seemed to be gagging on the tube that had been placed down his throat. I took a deep breath, leaned over the incubator and gave him a kiss. "Hi, honey, Mommy's here. It's going to be all right." I turned, looking at Leslie. I guess I figured she would have some wonderful words of wisdom for me. She did.

"He needs to hear your voice; it's really important. I've even asked the people in charge of social activities to play a tape of my voice for our little one. I'm sure you could do the same thing if you wanted to. That way, you wouldn't feel guilty if you have to leave. Remember, you have to take time out for yourself, and for the rest of your family."

Marcos' condition didn't improve at all that first week. The doctors told me his weight had gone down from the 8 pounds, 3 ounces to which I had nursed him, back down to 6 pounds, 7 ounces. They needed to somehow get more calories, more nutrients into his tiny body. The IV feedings just weren't enough.

They told me they needed to get permission from Marcos' social worker to do a surgical procedure. This procedure would involve placing a Broviac, or pump, above the heart, and this would have larger openings allowing thicker, richer nutrients to enter his depleted body. Whenever they needed to push almost anything through the IV, they could use the Broviac instead of poking him again and again.

When Marcos had aspirated those first few times, he evidently retained some of the fluid in his lungs. He developed a terrible case of pneumonia, and had to be placed on IV antibiotics. This would make it easier on him.

It took another week for them to get Marcos strong enough to even discuss the possibility of surgery. The specialist felt that Marcos needed surgery to correct the reflux from which he was suffering. If they could provide a G.T. tube through surgery, this could at least temporarily provide him with a way to get food to his stomach, until the surgery had a chance to heal.

It's strange, but when I think back to the time when first little Marcos was placed in our care, I can't believe they sent him out without at least a heart monitor and oxygen. Rumor has it that this was common practice for hospitals saddled with a county kid with no prospect of a home. If they could pass him off as "normal" then he would get placed.

Now, he was not only on a heart monitor, but also a ventilator and an oximeter. Personally, I liked the little oximeter. My Grandma Fern always said, "Always look for the good in everything." Well...the good I found was being able to smile when I saw a little red light that remained on Marcos' toe at all times. This little light registered how much oxygen he was absorbing. We actually gave Marcos the nickname of "Rudolph."

At the end of Marcos' third week in ICU, the doctors had decided we needed to start him gaining some serious weight. Here he was at seven months of age, only weighing eight pounds! The doctors decided that they should go ahead and do the surgical procedure to correct his esophagus. This way when Marcos would eat, his food would go down and stay down-quite the opposite of what it had been doing all his life!

We were told that Marcos was an extremely high-risk patient. He had a 50/50 chance of surviving the surgery. His whole life could end right on the operating table, or it could be the beginning of a much healthier existence.

The surgeons got the necessary papers signed by Marcos' social worker. They planned to start the operation at 7:00 a.m. I kissed Marcos goodnight, and told the nursing staff I would be back by 6:30 a.m. I tried to sleep through the night, but found myself tossing and turning most of the night. Because I had a restless night, I didn't hear the alarm go off. Dave, trying to be "helpful," decided to let me sleep in for a change.

I awakened at 6:45 a.m. When I realized the time, and the fact that I might never see Marcos alive again, I started grabbing whatever I could find to wear. I pulled on an old pair of blue jeans and a blouse hanging on the back of the bathroom door. I wasn't going to let Marcos down. I brushed my hair and applied make-up at stop signals on the way to the hospital. I took the diamond lane (designated for cars with two or more occupants), figuring I would chance getting a ticket. I wasn't going to miss seeing Marcos. I knew it was important for him to hear my voice and feel loved before he went into that operating room.

I arrived at the ICU floor at 7:05 a.m. and breathed a sigh of relief when I found he was still in his usual spot. They had been unable to leave for the operating room because they needed a respiratory therapist to push air into Marcos' lungs while he was being transported.

The technician who would be performing this task arrived about five minutes after I did.

Nurses were on either side of his incubator, the respiratory therapist by his head, and I was at his feet. We finally got started toward the elevators at 7:25 a.m. I was more relaxed by this time, just because I was finally there with Marcos.

We took the elevator down to the basement level of Children's Hospital. We took a large tunnel which ended up at the operating facilities of a neighboring hospital. I remembered reading about cases such as the Frustaci Septuplets, when they kept the mother in O.R. while they transferred the babies to neonatal ICU next door. This was my first experience with shared hospital facilities.

The surgeon arrived at the operating room doors, just as we exited the elevator. "Hi there, Mrs. Magnusen. Looks like he is ready to go." The doctor's tone was so cheery, I couldn't help but feel optimistic about the outcome of this surgery. "We'll be in there for about three hours. You can wait up in the front lobby area. They will let you know when he is back in ICU Because he's in ICU, he won't have to go to recovery first." The surgeon kept telling me all kinds of information. I just hoped he wasn't using up all his energy on me and our conversation.

Four and a half hours passed, and still there had been no word on Marcos' condition. I had had too much time to sit and think, and had come up with all kinds of ideas and fears. One could safely say my imagination was working overtime.

Five and a half hours passed. Finally I was given the news I had been awaiting: Marcos was all right. He was in ICU now, resting comfortably. I breathed a sigh of relief and headed toward that little angel's room. He looked basically the same, with the exception of two things. First, he had an additional tube coming out of his stomach. This was the tube that was going to provide nutrients for him until he was able to eat on his own. The second was another tube inserted through his nose and into his stomach. This tube would suction up any waste that collected in his stomach. The stomach had to have a complete rest until his esophagus had healed. He looked so pathetic. I asked myself, "Why does he keep fighting so hard?"

I eased myself into the rocking chair next to the incubator and sang quietly into his ear. I stayed for the rest of the day, then headed home to spend some time with the rest of the family.

The morning after surgery, I came into ICU, not expecting anything like what I was about to witness. Marcos had slept quite well during the night. He was progressing. He responded to my voice when

I sang to him, and tried to turn his head in my direction.

The nurse came over to his incubator and set up a tray with the syringes containing his painkiller, as well as the vitamin K shot that had been ordered for him. First to be injected into the Broviac was the vitamin K. She sterilized the entry area and slowly inserted the syringe. As the vitamin made its way into his body, Marcos turned purple, stiffening up straight as a board. All his alarms went off. His nurse started screaming, "Code blue! Code blue! I need a crash cart, STAT!" Wheels were set in motion. Doctors who had been working on other patients in the ward left what they were doing and ran to help Marcos survive. The crash cart was in place, and syringes were being loaded with many different medications.

Finally, someone noticed that I was standing in the background. I knew I had been there much longer than most parents would have been allowed to stay, and I knew I would have to leave. The social worker came over and escorted me to the waiting area. The tall, thin doctor who had been working on Marcos came over to me. My stomach tied in a knot as I waited to hear about Marcos' condition.

"We got him back, but it was close there for awhile." I couldn't believe that Marcos did it again. He had come so close to death so many times that I had quit counting.

Marcos' condition gradually improved. Social Services didn't feel they should let him come back to be with us because of insurance liability. Because he still had a tube in his tummy, he was considered to be extremely risky.

Update...

The county has placed Marcos in a state licensed foster home. He has now been living with his current family for over eight and a half years. The child who doctors said would never be more than a vegetable is able to see, hear and communicate with those around him. His foster family is hoping to adopt him, and says that he is much more than they ever dreamed he could be, and they are very happy things turned out this way.

I know in my heart that if Marcos could fight as hard as he did in the beginning, he will get where he is meant to go in life. There is definitely a reason for Marcos in our world!

Bejay

There had been a vacant spot in our home for two weeks after the marathon hospital duty with Marcos, and I was anxious to have someone to cuddle and care for. Since Brian was now a cool eight year old, and Lani was seven going on thirty, they weren't too keen on the idea of letting me rock and cuddle them, as an outlet for all my unused motherly feelings...

One cool autumn morning the call came I had been awaiting. "Hello, Debbe? This is Rhonda from ESH. We have a baby for you." "Oh...great!" I exclaimed. "I had about given up waiting-I was afraid they were never going to need me," I said rather sarcastically-knowing full well they were usually desperate for families to take children.

I was informed that the mother of this little one was in the mental unit of the county hospital. The father was a juvenile delinquent, currently serving time for attacking an officer. The plan was to place the baby with relatives who would be arriving in the near future.

My sister-in-law, Kirsten, was visiting that day, and since she is a registered nurse I thought she would appreciate seeing how babies were placed after leaving the hospital. We were both excited, but I'm sure I had her beat because we were going to pick up my new baby-of-the-week. As we approached the off-ramp a call on the car phone startled us. "Hi honey," my husband said. "I'm glad I caught you...uh, you better stop for gas. It's below empty." We coasted into a convenient station and I filled it with only as much as I needed in order to get to the shelter. I had been too excited to even notice the need for fuel.

There, in a small area designated for official visits between children and their birth parents, I saw one of the workers holding a small bundle in her arms. "Hi, Debbe, let's go into my office and sign the papers," Betty suggested. We walked over to the desk and she handed me the baby. "Here, go ahead and hold him-I need to add one thing to this report," she said. I lifted the blanket and took a quick peek. "Can we go into the waiting area and sit down?" "Sure," Betty agreed, so I handed the baby over to Kirsten and we all walked to the waiting area. I finished signing the papers and took a second look at the baby. I was hoping I would find my first glimpse had been a mistake...

I joked to Kirsten: "Gosh...I wouldn't be a bit surprised if his parents are ET and Yoda." To myself I added, "Boy, I'm sure glad this one is leaving soon. I wouldn't want anyone to think he's mine."

We carried him out to the car and headed for the department store. He slept the entire way, but somehow found time to mess his diaper. We placed him on a clean mat in the trunk of the Seville. The

Baby's plumbing worked just fine. After a quick diaper change, (which he didn't like one bit), we entered the store.

This was always one of my favorite times in getting a new baby. Picking out just the right blanket-the one you knew they would some-day drag along the ground behind them...the blanket that would cause tears to come to that child's eyes when it could not be found. That was special. You wouldn't be able to go with that child to his next home, but the blanket would. I also routinely selected a special kimono for each baby. When they outgrew it, I would attach a little note that would read something like this: "You wore this when you came home from the hospital; hope you keep this kimono for your future child, when you grow up and get married." I would include a photo of the child in the outfit.

The whole family came down to greet little Bejay. A tradition had started with our first child. We always took a Polaroid photo of each baby as they came into the house. This was placed on the refrigerator. Each day when I go into the kitchen I see their faces, reminding me to say a prayer for them. I don't know where they all are, but I feel God has His hands on them.

Bejay was very different from the other babies we had cared for. He would not look at anyone. You could try to force him to look at you, but he would deliberately look in the opposite direction. He re-fused to be cuddled, and made no attempt to smile or coo. He wanted absolutely nothing to do with the real world.[1]

It wasn't until a fellow foster-mom saw Bejay that I began to piece together what was wrong with him. She made me aware of abnor-malities she saw in his behavior, and explained she had had a child with similar symptoms when they first got her. It helped me under-stand why Bejay had been so hard to get to love. He rejected the love I had to give-and he didn't want love from anyone else either, for that matter.

By the time Bejay was three months old, he seemed to lack all the basic essentials to develop any sort of bond.[2] The child who was going to stay for a few weeks had now been with us for three months. During this time, we discovered his mother had taken three different drugs for her schizophrenia-(a psychosis characterized by disassocia-tion from the environment, and deterioration of her personality.)

We also learned that the child's father had a violent past. When he was only eight years old, he evidently became upset with his mother and decided, while she lay in bed, recuperating from surgery, to set her bed on fire while she was in it. (He did awaken her to let her know the bed was on fire before it was too late...)

I began working with Bejay, as did the rest of the family. After four days of placing him on our bed, holding our hands on either side of his face so he had no choice but to look at us, we made a major break-through. We also made sure, when feeding him, that there was no place else to look except to the care-giver. No eye contact...no bottle. The nipple went back in his mouth when he would look at me for even a moment. Then he was acknowledging my presence.

We had taken the entire family down to the Bay to watch the Christmas boat parade when all of a sudden Bejay started babbling. I looked at my daughter, then she looked over the back seat of the car to see where this strange sound was coming from. Neither of us could believe it was Bejay. We were so excited. finally, all our hard work had paid off.

We celebrated Christmas Eve at Dave's parent's home, and passed the baby from person to person. He was fed by relatives, cradled by all, but something we were very unaware of was taking place during that holiday party. Bejay, somehow, felt he was again being rejected. He regressed to the same glazed, detached state in which he had been previously.

We were getting ready to leave for a two-week vacation and decided we had better take Bejay with us. We had our work cut out for us. After four more days of non-stop work and love, we were able to get this little guy back to smiling, cooing and babbling, and we succeeded in getting him to look at us during his feedings. It made the rest of our trip so enjoyable. We still have the photo of his first smile. To most, it just looks like the average kid smiling-but to us, it means the beginning of life for Bejay. This little guy was probably going to join the land of the living, instead of being institutionalized. Perhaps he would even enjoy life!

God works in some very unique and wonderful ways. Throughout this book, I think you will see how God has used little Bejay.

Update...

Since Bejay first came into our home, we have learned that his beauty is on the inside; he just needed someone to love him, so this beauty could come out. This little boy has a personal key to our hearts. He asks the blessing at the dinner table, and thanks God for the monorail at Disneyland every night.

Bejay is no longer a ward of the court. After two and a half years of foster care, he was put up for adoption. Would you like to guess who adopted him? That's right-WE DID! We love him so very much, and have had the pleasure of watching him blossom. The doctors have marveled at Bejay's progress. The thought of where he could have ended up if we had been closed to other's suggestions is a frightening one to contemplate.

They say that when you live with someone, you begin to look like them. Well...Bejay has my blue/green eyes, his big sister's golden brown hair, the shape of his big brother's face, and his Dad's plumbing. I still say he was "unique" at birth, but now he is so adorable. Look out, Burt Reynolds!

The "Green Baby"

At the beginning of this chapter I introduced you to Marcos. Every birthday I sent him something, as well as a family photo at Christmas. Four holiday seasons had come and gone without a word from Marcos-but I realized his current foster mom didn't have time to respond, as she had many children with high needs in her care. I had always carried memories of Marcos in my mind, but I just hadn't felt I could go visit him quite yet. But all this changed the Christmas of 1989.

I had received a new baby in the middle of November, and knew from day one that this was going to be a challenge. This child had been born exposed to cocaine and amphetamines. He wasn't as fortunate as most of my other babies, because he also suffered from a malformed heart. This frail little baby had to try to gain enough weight so that he could survive at least two open heart operations.

I had arrived at the ESH office to sign the release papers, after going over them with the head social worker. I was handed five different medications as well, with specific notes like "This Rx to be taken at 8 a.m. and 8 p.m.-VERY CRITICAL", or "Watch for BLUE around the mouth..."

Now this last instruction I found a bit comical. This baby was black as the night. How was I supposed to tell if he was blue? I ended up calling a local baby hot-line, and learned it's best to check under the baby's tongue to see if it has turned blue, or check the bed of his fingernails. Now, this made more sense!

I took all fifty pages of medical history and little Rodney out to the van. The only way I could convince the three foster toddlers to get in their car seats was to allow each of them to come give Rodney a kiss and a hug first. All three little ones added a rub on his head as well-something about all those little curls pressed tightly against his tiny head was irresistible.

When Bejay, our now three-year old adopted son, came into our bedroom the morning after Rodney's arrival, he climbed up onto our bed where I sat feeding Rodney. He said, "Mom, I LIKE this green baby." He rubbed the tiny curls with the palm of his hand and said, "Let's get another green one, too." Dave and I tried not to chuckle out loud, but it was tough. Our son knew that there was some color difference, and he also knew that green was a color - so...he figured out that at least he would try and name a color that sounded right, so Dad and Mom would know what he meant. Many a day we found this precious three-year old standing next to Rodney's bassinet, silently looking at the "little green baby." He would rest Rodney's head on his one hand and rub his

40

curls with the other. He would stand perfectly still for long periods of time, just watching that tiny baby working so hard to breathe...

After a visit to a pediatric cardiologist, it was determined that Rodney was in congestive heart failure to some degree, and it was going to take close monitoring in order to succeed in getting him to surgery.

We had three medication changes in the last week of November and the first week of December. We also had two visits to the hospital. The first was a brief one to the ER The following day another medication change was ordered, and the week following went fairly smoothly.

The second time Rodney needed medical attention was not quite as simple as the first time. That particular December morning dawned cold and blustery. We had enjoyed two and a half weeks watching Rodney improve, with the wonderful help of Dr. W. Singer and his staff. We thanked God for each and every day that we were allowed to be with him, but this particular day when he awoke at 5 a.m., I could sense that there was something very wrong with Rodney, and realized I might need help.

By noon, Rodney's frail body shook as he gasped desperately for each breath. I got in touch with his cardiologist and we devised a plan to change his medication. Now all we could do was to wait and pray for an improvement. But he failed to get better. His respiration rate reached 120 breaths per minute, and the doctor concluded we had no choice but to put him into the Intensive Care Unit.

Shortly after this decision was made, I got a phone call from the hospital: "I'm sorry, Mrs. Magnusen, this is the registration office at the hospital and we thought we had better let you know that at this time, there are no beds available. If you could please keep him there at home, we will probably have space available by 5:30 this evening."

What could I say...I had no real choice. Of course I was going to keep him there at home and watch him like a hawk! Yep, that's what I was going to do.

As I sat cradling Rodney to my breast, I heard the scurrying of the other children's feet, as they all tried to get to the mail which had just come through the mail slot. (Why this seemed to be the biggest single event in our daily schedule, I'll never know...) Lani brought that portion of the mail she had grabbed, and in it was a letter with an unfamiliar return address. I noticed a "Do Not Bend" written on the outside, and decided to open that envelope first.

Inside the envelope was a 5" x 7" photograph of a beautiful little boy, smiling from ear to ear. The love in his eyes beamed through to the viewer. The straps that held Marcos in the wheelchair only covered a small portion of his red, white and blue T-shirt. Tears welled up in my eyes as I realized the identity of the little boy in that photograph. I couldn't believe the timing that God provided. He knew that I felt as though I was going through the same scenario all over again with Rodney: the uncertainty of whether or not this child was going to make it to his first birthday; wondering if he would ever be well enough to run in the park, or eat a hot dog at a ball game. Would Rodney have to go through as much pain and suffering as had Marcos?

I felt that God wanted me to see this photo, as I waited for a hospital bed for Rodney. It was God's way of telling me to hang in there-we had done it before, we could do it again!

The call finally came, and we were allowed to take Rodney to ICU. As I filled out all the normal paperwork and walked the familiar hallways, I saw faces that I had seen four years before. It was almost like being back home. A part of the familiarity felt good, because I knew all the basics, and knew what was expected of me. On the other hand, that familiarity also brought feelings of unrest. I questioned myself as to whether or not they would decide that Rodney was too high-risk to come back with us. I kept the beautiful photograph of Marcos in my mind, and knew in my heart that whatever the outcome was going to be, I wasn't the one in control. I would do the best I could, while Rodney was my foster child, to see that he knew he was loved and cared for, just as I had with Marcos.

Four days passed before Rodney became stable enough that the doctors were willing to release him back to us. We were now on two new medications, and looking pretty darn good!

The following two weeks were wonderful. We got to enjoy the beautiful "green baby" as he began to grow. The reward of seeing an extremely sick child as he begins to coo, and to smile that very first smile-those moments are irreplaceable. But after those two really good weeks, Rodney did end up back in the hospital. We kept our hopes high, hoping that he would soon be returning home.

I can honestly tell you that this is the one part of being a foster parent that is hardest for me to deal with. You see, at this point in time-(two days before Christmas)-I was told that I would not be taking Rodney back home. Instead, he would be going to another foster home where there were no other children, and a licensed nurse would be taking the title of foster mom. It was extremely hard for me to let Rodney go, especially since we hadn't finished what we had started out to accomplish. We felt that since we had helped keep him alive this long, we should be able to see him through his surgery.

As I write, Rodney is still in intensive care, on life support. He just had major open heart surgery that hopefully will solve his problems. It will be a long road to travel before we know if Rodney will survive...

No matter whether he lives or dies, he will always hold a special spot in our hearts, as he was our special "green baby".

Update...

The little "green baby" lives. It has been almost two years since Rodney went through open heart surgery. Rodney spent five weeks on life support, just fighting for his life. Eventually they felt that there was no other option but to go ahead with the procedure. The risk was running higher every day the operation was postponed.

I received a call in the past month from the family who fostered Rodney after we were taken off the case. I am pleased to announce that Rodney is in the midst of being adopted by this wonderful family. It's so much easier to let them go, when you know they're going to be O.K.!

Sara

I love being a foster parent...and that's the truth! It's been a dream come true for me. When I was just a little girl, I started taking in abandoned kittens, puppies, squirrels, etc. After reaching my teen years, I graduated into caring for tarantulas and opossums.

When I met my husband, Dave, all that changed. I realized how very precious each human life is, and decided to put more of my energies toward helping human beings. Dave and I decided before we got married that we would only have two children of our own, then we would either adopt children or become foster parents. We felt that instead of complaining about the problems of this world, we should try to do something to solve them. If we could take one child off the streets or out of an orphanage, and make him/her feel worthy of being somebody, then we should do just that.

We encountered many babies whose mothers had passed drugs into the child they carried. One of these babies was extremely near and dear to my heart. I'll call her Sara, and this is her story.

June 10, 1987: I'm twenty minutes late picking up the newest member of our family. As I walk through the doors to Orangewood, Regina Mayor frantically runs toward me. "Where have you been-you're late!" "Traffic held me up. Sorry," I replied. As soon as we heard the "buzz" of the security button, we quickly walked down the hall toward her office. As we walked, Regina informed me that Beverly Jacobs, her co-worker, had the baby in her arms and couldn't get her to stop crying. The familiar high-pitched screams of a baby going through drug withdrawal gets louder and louder.

There was a look of panic on Beverly's face, as she cradled the baby and tried to figure out what she was doing wrong. "Oh good-you're here. Do something to help! - I can't get her to stop crying." I carefully took the baby from Beverly's arms and placed her on the desk. "I think we'd better check the diaper first, to see if that's the problem. It might turn out that she is suffering from the withdrawal symptoms of cocaine addiction, and we'll just have to get used to that scream."

"Boy, I can't imagine listening to that sound all the time," Regina said, as I continued to work on the baby. "Well, you just learn to shut the sound out of your mind, after awhile. It's really not so bad if you remember it does improve with time," I told them. Beverly said she was just going to stick with helping animals - and for her, I think that's perfect.

"What's her name?" I asked Bev, as I continued to remove the soiled diaper. "Oh, you get to name this one." I'd never heard this one before. "What?" I stopped in the midst of wiping a raw, bleeding bottom. "What do you mean?" "Oh, didn't I tell you...this one was abandoned in the hospital," Beverly said without batting an eye. I, on the other hand, was really taken aback by this information.

After tightly swaddling the five-pound bundle, I said, "What about Tiffany or Crystal...?" Regina cut in: "No way. That's what all the drug moms are naming their babies. Crystal is another name for the drugs they use." After backing down for a moment, I got nerve enough to suggest one more name. "How about Sara?" Not a complaint in the room...so...Sara it was. I quickly picked up a little bag which held her belongings - consisting of hospital soaps and diapers - and anxiously retreated to my car. When I reached home and introduced her to the family, she was still sleeping from the ride home and continued to sleep through every, single introduction.

Once Sara had met everyone, I needed to get on with the next order of business...The Bath. This is something no newborn relishes, but a task that must be done. As I unwrapped her, Sara's body began to stiffen and shake. She screamed from the shock of the cool air hitting her body. Upon close examination I saw that this baby had a horrible problem with her skin. Her entire body was peeling. Scales began to peel away from every inch of her torso and limbs. She had open, bleeding wounds on both feet. Evidently her skin had gotten so dry that fissures opened. One on her left foot started to ooze pus. I gently washed off the open sores on her fragile skin with hydrogen peroxide and finished by giving her a sponge bath. I swabbed the umbilical cord with alcohol, then applied a soothing lotion over the greatest part of her body. Unfortunately many drug babies suffer from excessively dry skin, as well as from bloody bottoms. Withdrawal symptoms come from chemicals stored in the fatty cells of the baby's liver, which doesn't start to function till after birth.

Sara spent her first Easter with us, and as she started filling out and stopped scaling we found ourselves falling in love with this little baby doll. In my heart, she had already become a daughter to me. Sara had nobody, and we were sure she would stay.

God had a different plan for Sara. Our children-Lani and Brian, had been home-schooled for the previous two years. I had hired a tutor to work with them on a weekly basis. When their tutor, Caty, came over for her weekly visit, I showed off my ten day old bundle. I had just recently learned that Caty and her husband, Mark, had been trying for nine years to have a family. They had tried all the usual remedies, as well as an infertility specialist, but nothing seemed to help. As Caty sat, tutoring the children at the dining room table, I gently placed Sara in Caty's arms. "Here...maybe this will work." I told her as I stepped back to view this beautiful scene. "What are you talking about?" Caty chuckled, as she looked down at the little angel sleeping in her arms. "You know-maybe if you hold her, something will rub off, and you'll get pregnant," I told her.

"Oh, I'd love to take her, but with Mark being a policeman, he isn't willing to work with the system." "We'll see," I smirked. Caty didn't know me that well-she didn't realize that when I feel something is right, I go for it-and I definitely felt this was "right."

After Caty left, I placed a quick call to her house, hoping that Mark would answer the phone. Although we had met only in passing a couple of times, I felt if I used the right approach, I could at least get Sara's foot in the door.

On the fourth ring someone picked up the phone. "Hello?" boomed a big, deep voice. "Hi Mark, this is Debbe. I just had a question for Caty. Could you leave her the message?" "Sure. What is it?" Now I had him. His curiosity was aroused. "Well, I have a beautiful little foster baby here who needs a good home. I thought maybe you and Caty might have some names of people that might be interested."

"Maybe WE would be," Mark said. "Oh. Well, okay, why don't you and Caty talk it over, and if you're serious about it I'll tell you the next steps." Within twenty-four hours I received a phone call which changed Sara's future.

They decided they would like to try to become Sara's foster parents. If the mother was unable to reunify with her daughter, whom she had abandoned in the hospital, then possibly Mark and Caty would be able to give Sara a permanent home. I had mixed emotions about their decision. I knew it would be great for Sara, but a part of me would miss her very much. If it was meant to be, I knew the Lord would help me get over this mountain, and on to the next one...

Because Sara was a high risk baby, born exposed to cocaine, she began to show more of the symptoms associated with drug withdrawal. She was trembling so much she burned up all the calories she was able to consume. Instead of using an ordinary nipple for her formula, we had to use juice nipples. The sucking desire is strong, but the actual force a drug -exposed baby is able to exert is minimal. She began to lose weight, so she was placed on Phenobarbital, to reduce her tremors.

When it came time to transfer Sara to her new home, it was very important that this move take place gradually. It can be so detrimental to move a child abruptly that some never recuperate from the ordeal. They go through the rest of their lives saying to themselves: "Why did

I love them so much? It hurts so bad now that they are gone, so I'm never going to let myself get that close again." Dr. Ken Magid and Carole McKelvey, authors of High Risk-Children Without A Conscience, reiterate this phenomenon. I recommended this book to Mark and Caty, and they, too, found it extremely helpful in understanding how to deal with a child who is being moved.

After one month of visiting with Sara, Caty and Mark brought their video camera to film their new foster child as she was carried to their car and strapped into her new car seat.

In the months following, Mark and Caty spent much of their time performing physical therapy with Sara and tending her needs. How this child improved with their loving care! They knew Sara was already at risk for cerebral palsy, due to damage to her central nervous system-but her chances for normal development were greatly improved due to their loving care and strong bonding. The first few times I visited Sara after she moved away, tears came to my eyes-but God has been good to me and has taken my hurt away.

Mark and Caty privately adopted another little girl during the first year of Sara's foster care. They realized there was a possibility that Sara might go back to her birth mother. In addition, Caty became pregnant-so in twenty-four months they had Sara, barely two, Bethanny, turning one, and newborn Taylor, their son!

When Sara had been in foster care for eighteen months, the time came for her PPH or Permanency Planning Hearing. The social worker on their case was about to go on maternity leave and so a new social worker, unfamiliar with details, wrote the required report in the month before the hearing.

The report she wrote did not look very hopeful for Mark and Caty. It had no mention of the birth mother's failure to complete parenting classes. It did not mention that she had dropped out of drug testing two months prior to the hearing. Nor did it mention that she failed to show up during half the scheduled visits to see Sara. (The mother claimed that she couldn't come because her car had broken down-and she quit her job because of a lack of transportation. With no job, there was no possibility of getting the car fixed...so...she failed to keep her appointments!)

Mark and Caty retained the services of an attorney, so that they might protect Sara's rights. As the contested hearing date approached, the mother became frightened by the appearance of the extra attorney, as well as that of an investigator who had been put on the case. Just two weeks before the hearing was to take place, Sara's birth mother miraculously decided to give her up. She signed the papers required for her to relinquish her rights as Sara's mother.

It has been almost a year since that signature was written, yet Sara has not been freed for adoption. The reason: the father has left the state and he has to be given the chance to either sign off or to appear in court to state his choices in regard to parenting.

Update...

Guess who just got adopted...that's right, little Sara! She was the first to arrive at Mark and Caty's home, but the last to legally join the family. She is dearly loved by one and all.

I hate to admit it but I cried at her adoption ceremony. After it was over I explained to Sara's new family the reason. I knew that I really wanted to keep Sara, and came very close to being selfish rather than handing her over to Mark and Caty. But if I had done this, Sara would have probably gone back to her birth mother. Caty's family could afford the legal advice and private detective that I couldn't have paid for. By my following God's guidance, Sara has the chance of growing up in a wonderful loving home.

James

The next case started out much rockier, but had a much simpler ending.

With less than five hours sleep, I stumbled out of bed. I wondered what this crazy day would bring. No two days are ever the same.

Who was hungry? Would I basically just play the role of mom or would I be confronted by a crazed or drugged parent, trying to "protect" their child...Would a social worker give me a call, telling me he was hoping to come by in the next few hours for a monthly visit with one of the children...

I reached for the clanging phone in time to hear a very chipper voice say, "Good morning, Debbe, this is Melinda." Melinda was a petite woman who dressed as if she was always on her way to an important business meeting. I knew from past experience that Melinda was excellent at investigative work, and that she tried very hard to get her case work completed and handed over to the court on time. Her decision could be-and usually was-the primary paperwork read by the judge. Her report could be the determining factor in many cases. I was glad she took her job so seriously.

"Is it really going to be a good one? I'm allergic to mornings," I complained as I wiped the sleep from my half-opened eyes.

"Oh, come on, Debbe," she chuckled. "You know you love it. Why else would you put yourself in line for all these babies?" I was glad Melinda knew me well enough to realize I was only joking. I still dream about sleeping in, but that's usually as far as it goes: just dreaming. And that's okay with me!

With her best sales pitch technique, Melinda enthused: "I think I have a case for you. I know you were looking for another baby, and I have a family who is desperately looking for a family from their church. You see, they're Mormon. As of yet, I haven't been able to locate anyone, so I told them you were a real nice Christian family. So if you could just reassure the mom when she calls, I'd really appreciate it. Then we could place tomorrow."

I wondered why these people would care whether we were Mormon or not. If they were "in the system," why would they care at all? An extremely high percentage of all the parents we had ever encountered could not have cared less about what day it was, or if there was food in the house, let alone where their children were placed...

"What's this one's background?" I asked. "I mean, is this a cocaine baby?" "Nope. We're sending you something a bit different this time." A few moments of silence passed, then she turned on her best salesman tone of voice. "This little guy's cute as a bug," she began. "His name is James, and well...he's been in Intensive Care Unit at Children's for the past five days. He had a cerebral hemorrhage behind the left eye. He was having seizures, and now he's on medication to control them. It seems to be working."

"What happened...I mean...why the hemorrhage?"

"The doctors say, a trauma like that had to come from somebody. Either he was beaten or dropped, or somebody shook him harder than you or I could ever imagine. Personally, I don't think the parents did it. My gut feeling on this one is that they're clean."

"Well, sure, I guess we can take him. Let me put it to a family vote, but since I know they have all been wanting another one, I can't imagine they will vote no. Sure enough, everyone agreed. I called Melinda back with the news, then heard her say, "Great! I'll get the paperwork started and let you know later today exactly when we'll be out."

"Oh, by the way...what about visitations?" I asked.

"The usual one hour per week, but I think this mom is not going to handle it too well. I'll tell you what...you use your own judgment, and see what you think. If you don't mind her being there more, it's fine with me." That's what I really like about Melinda. Even though I might be "just a foster parent" to many, I was a respected co-worker in Melinda's eyes. I trusted Melinda's evaluation, and I hoped to prove her right.

On a hazy February afternoon, one of Social Services placement workers, Regina Mayor, carefully brought an overloaded car seat to the front door. Brian and Lani hid behind the double dutch doors to the dining room the moment Regina rang the bell. They were anxious to see the new little bundle, but not as anxious for the social worker to know it.

Regina gently placed the car seat containing a beautiful sleeping baby on our dining room table. As she began to assemble the papers for me to sign, I gently undid the straps on the seat. James looked up with his big, brown eyes long enough to take a lazy peek at his surroundings, then drifted back into sleep.

James' dark black hair was so clean and neatly cut. He was definitely not deprived of food, either. He had a husky build. There were no bruises on his body, and he had a nice tan skintone that most beach goers would die for.

Our daughter, Lani, was eight at that time, and she was very curious to find out more about our newest guest. She brought along Bejay, our bug-eyed three-month old foster baby for company.

I wondered what the parents would be like. Were they like so many of the others we had met? Would they skip from job to job, lie to lie, never leaving a forwarding address? Only time would tell. The first time I met James' mother was two days after he had been placed with us.

When I opened the door, she introduced herself with a thick Brazilian accent. I invited her in and she immediately made a bee-line for James. He was very excited to see her. They had so much fun, I decided to allow her to stay for the rest of the afternoon. She fed him (and he ate better than ever before)-cuddled, talked to him, etc. This was a very loving relationship. The father arrived at 4:30 in the afternoon. James went directly to him, giggled and responded to this gentle man. They both stayed long enough to feed him again and bathe him.

When they prepared to leave, I asked if they would like to come back the next day. They were both surprised, and pleased. The father explained that he had to work, but it was fine with him if Mom came, as long as she wouldn't be imposing.

When she arrived the next day she told me that she had slept much better after her visit with us. She even brought diapers, food and blankets for the baby. This was definitely a first for me...

For the next month, we spent lots of time together with James' parents, Rob and Vona. Our goal was to keep James' bond to his parents very strong. It turned out that the charges were dropped, and no one was blamed. I still feel the baby's mistreatment was due to the baby-sitter.

The sad part about this whole story is that Vona didn't have to work. She wanted to take James to Brazil to see her father. This was the first grandson; she and Rob had tried for many years to have a child. The extra money she made at work was to pay for their flight to Brazil. By the time they got through paying court costs, after being found not guilty, they had to postpone their trip.

Vona and I still remain friends. We have been friends for over four years and I have no doubt that Melinda's "gut feelings" were right all along.

GOODBYE, FOSTER CHILD
by Debbe Magnusen

Not flesh of our flesh, nor bone of our bones,
But yet in our hearts and our lives you have grown.
I send you now freely to a new home for care,
And pray for your safety as long as you're there.
A place in my heart will not be the same-
It will now skip a beat, when I hear your name.
You may not remember the time that we shared,
But I want you to know just how much we cared.
There were nights that were long; days like that too.
But it bound us together: what a team, me and you.
As I wave when you leave, my tears I'll hold back
And remember I gave you the home that you lacked.
Not flesh of my flesh, nor bone of my bones,
But forever the memory of you I will own.

Don't Mess with Big Mama!

Most foster mothers face challenges on a daily basis. I am certainly not the only one who has gone through many trials and tribulations.

Sometimes foster parents are given a child who does not want to live. They must hold that child for hours on end, trying to force feed him, to make him aware that he is loved. Eventually, the foster parents are rewarded for their efforts by seeing that child begin to fight for himself.

Sometimes foster parents are fighting the system for simple things-like obtaining a medical card or records. To most people, this doesn't seem like a big problem. But when you are caring for a drug-exposed baby who is considered to be "high risk," you need that card in order to get medical treatment. One never knows when a child might have to be rushed to the hospital in need of emergency care. I can remember one time when the plan which I considered best for a particular child was one which completely differed from the plan the social worker advocated. I had to fight to get my voice heard, but only through the help of a national organization called CASA (Court Appointed Special Advocates), were we able to protect that child. I had to petition the court, to ask that they appoint a CASA representative to the case. It takes time to learn how the system works, and it takes willingness by the care giver to seek answers that sometimes lie undiscovered.

Before I took my first foster child, I was considered to be a very passive person. I tried desperately to find ways to get things done without ruffling anyone's feathers. Since taking on my first tough case, I have had a complete change of personality. I am constantly trying to find ways to get things done for the sake of the children. A dear girlfriend, Nellie Tilton, knew me back in the old days. She had been away with her husband in the service. When she returned, she saw the "new me," and she sat in shock as I voiced my opinion about a child and his needs, and exactly how things needed to be done.

When I got off the phone, Nellie said, "Wow! I can't believe that's you. You never would have stood up to anyone like that before."

I was actually startled by her comment. I had never thought about what I was doing. I only did what seemed to come naturally. I turned and looked at Nellie and said, "Well, don't mess with BIG MAMA." We both laughed, and after that I began to realize that when anything gets in the way of a child receiving the best counseling, therapy, treatment, or respect he or she deserves, we foster mothers will fight back. Our hearts are in the right places. No, we definitely don't get involved in foster care for the money. There is no amount of money that could pay for all the emotional ups and downs that we sometimes encounter.

I have learned that the vast majority of foster parents out there have experienced many situations that are interesting, challenging and rewarding. I have compiled just a few of their wonderful stories for this book. You can be assured that every person mentioned in this book is only a small part of a much larger group of caring, loving human beings who have had to deal with similar situations. The stories contained in this chapter are true but cities, names, dates and identifications of many have been changed for the safety and privacy of the people I interviewed.

The Paper Bag Baby

In the summer of 1981 Mrs. Jenny Johnson rode her bike along the streets of her little town, just as she had every morning for the previous ten years. She had started her day with her cup of decaf and a bran muffin, then pulled her bike out of the garage to go on the usual three-mile ride. Everything seemed to be going like clockwork. She passed Thelma, the school crossing guard, as she crossed Euclid Avenue at the usual time, in her usual way.

As she turned into the back alley of the local five-and-dime, she saw something out of the corner of her eye that was not a part of her usual routine. It was a large, brown paper bag...and the bag was moving. This aroused Jenny's curiosity, and she just had to turn her bike around, and find out what was in that sack. She climbed off the bike, kicked the kick-stand into place, and bent over to open the bag as it moved again. Jenny was startled by this and she jumped back a bit, before continuing to open the crumpled end.

As she opened the mouth of the bag, she got the shock of her life. There, in the bottom of the bag, lay a brand new baby girl. The umbilical cord was still partially connected, and blood and vernix covered this child from head to toe. It was the only thing protecting her from the outside elements of this cruel world.

Jenny quickly lifted the little baby out of the bag and ran to the front of the store. She wrapped the baby in the sweat shirt she had draped over her shoulders. She had to call 9-1-1 quickly. She pounded on the front door of the dime store. Someone had to hear her-this was one time the normally shy woman had to assert herself.

Mr. Peters moseyed to the front door, when he realized it was Jenny. He wondered where her bike was - maybe it had been stolen, he thought. Better go ahead and humor the lady, since she was a regular customer. As he got closer to the front door, he realized Jenny had something in her arms. He clumsily tried to extract the key from his back pocket - the key that would unlock lots of juicy information! Maybe it would be the kind that would make the local paper. He could see it now. Yes, sir, this was gonna be a big one.

"Thank God you're here. Quick, get me a blanket for this poor little thing and hurry!" Jenny exclaimed. "Where's your phone?" We have to call for help!" Jenny followed Mr. Peters to his office. The baby was not very big, and she was afraid that it might not survive much longer without proper medical attention. The baby was making faint, squeaking sounds. Was she all right or not?

Jenny cradled the baby close to her chest as she heard the familiar sound of sirens in the background. For once, Jenny was relieved to hear them. She looked at the baby-was it wishful thinking, or was she actually getting a little bit more color in her frail, tiny body?

First on the scene was Officer John Byron. He had heard over his police radio that there was an abandoned infant in desperate need of attention. From the trunk of his car he took out the large white box with the Red Cross insignia on the lid. He hoped there would be something in it to help until the paramedics arrived. As he ran through the front door, Jenny made her way up the aisle. "How is it?" asked Officer Byron.

"I don't know. I sure hope she's gonna be..." Jenny's voice trailed off.

"Here, let me take a look. Wow! She fits in the palm of my hand! Here, little lady, let's change your outfit," the big man said. He pulled the emergency thermal blanket out of his kit and wrapped it tightly around the tiny body. The baby limply sagged into whatever position it was placed. Glancing at Jenny, the officer said, "There! You needed to have something warmer than that sporty sweat shirt." A little cough came from beneath the blanket. "Boy, I hope you haven't caught cold. You certainly don't need that," he said. He was starting to feel himself being drawn in by this little person. It was great to be needed and wanted. Most of the time, policemen have to put up cold exteriors, so as to be less vulnerable to the cruel realities of their work.

Lights and sirens brought the paramedics to the five-and-dime. They jumped from the cab of their truck and quickly hoisted two medical supply boxes from the side cabinets attached to the bed of the truck. When they walked briskly inside, they found a small group huddled at the front cash register of the store. "Oh Hi, John. Fancy meeting you here," the taller of the two paramedics said. "What do we have on this little one?"

"Well, it seems this little lady got stuffed in a paper bag, instead of an incubator. From what I've been able to tell, she seems to be coming around a bit since I wrapped her in this thermal blanket-wouldn't you agree, Mrs. Johnson?"

"Yes, I think you're right." Mrs. Johnson nodded her head.

The shorter, stockier paramedic was Brad Cline. Brad was fairly new on the job. This was his first chance to use all the techniques he had learned about emergency care of a newborn. He quickly set up the portable command post, enabling him and his partner, Lee, to communicate with the hospital that would be admitting this patient. While Brad worked, Lee continued to ask questions of both Jenny and Officer Byron. There was so little to go on, Lee became frustrated with what he was required to ask. When Brad had established radio contact with the hospital, the paramedics were instructed to set up an IV to keep the baby from dehydrating. They began to feel good about the baby's condition. They knew she was not out of the woods completely, but felt she had a fair, fighting chance, thanks to Jenny's alert eye. Despite the fact that logically, they were not to get emotionally involved with their patients, they still felt drawn to this helpless little child. Brad wondered who her parents were, while Lee speculated as to what the future was going to hold for her.

Ten days after Paper Bag Baby was admitted to the hospital, she was released to a wonderful foster mother and father. She weighed in at 4 pounds, 1 ounce, and was now up to 4 pounds, 14 ounces. She had been found when she was four hours old, a piece of umbilical cord still attached, which appeared to have been chewed off. The baby had been given a course of antibiotics intravenously, to protect her from possible infection.

For over a year, she stayed in the loving home of Mom and Dad Hoover. They nourished this child, both mentally and physically. They found her development somewhat delayed, and to this day are not sure if this was because she was born prematurely or whether it was due to her frightening first hours at birth.

When it came time for Paper Bag Baby to be placed in a permanent home, it was with heavy hearts that they carried her up the stairs of the adoption agency. At the time this placement was made, the adoption agency frowned greatly upon foster parents and adoptive parents getting together. They had the new family come in through an alternate entrance, a few minutes after the Hoovers arrived. The social worker took the baby into her arms, which greatly upset the baby, as well as the foster parents. The baby was carried into the room where her new family anxiously awaited her arrival. Most mothers would probably agree with me that the normal reaction would be for the adoptive mother to anxiously reach for this little infant, expecting to cradle and caress this gift from God. Unfortunately, Paper Bag Baby had other ideas. She knew that the only mother and father she had ever known were in some other room, and she wanted to be back with them...and NOW!

After half an hour of continual screaming, the adoptive parents asked if the agency could possibly get in touch with the foster parents. There had to be some way to calm down this frightened child, they reasoned. When the family was told that the foster parents were still in another room, the new parents demanded, "Why don't you bring them in here, for goodness sake? This poor child is scared to death. She needs her Mommy."

The startled worker went back into the main office, and when she reappeared with Mommy Hoover, the baby lunged toward her crying, "Mama! Mama!" She clung to the only mother she knew. As Mommy Hoover sat with the baby in her arms, it felt so good to both of them. This was the way they both wished it could be, but God, in His infinite wisdom, knew what was best for everyone.

The new parents suggested they should come to Baby's house-to the home with which she was familiar. If they expected to win her over, it would have to be on her own turf, and on her terms.

Two days after their frustrating first encounter, they arrived at Baby's home with a pocketful of prayers, and rejuvenated hope. Mommy Hoover had the bright idea of placing raisins in a cup, then handing this to the adoptive mother. There was a trail starting back where Baby first sat, leading all the way to Baby's new Mom. Slowly, cautiously, Baby toddled over to the cup containing the remaining raisins. After this initial investment of time, Baby built a ground level of trust with her new parents. At the end of the next visit, she left the Hoover's home for good. This was what the county felt was "in Baby's best interest."

Almost immediately the new parents invited Mom and Dad Hoover to visit-but the pain was still too real, especially for Mom Hoover. She asked that they give her three months to adjust, and for Baby to become accustomed to her new home. She didn't want to set herself and Baby up for an emotional high that would eventually have to end. It was this ending that scared her most. But finally, to satisfy her curiosity, Mom Hoover decided to place the long-awaited call. The three months had passed, and the family was extremely happy to hear from her.

The following Sunday Mom and Dad Hoover drove up to the house Baby now called home. The front yard was filled with flowers of assorted colors and sizes. The aroma of narcissus filled the air as they walked up the sidewalk. Before they could reach the front porch, the screen swung open and out came Baby and her mother. Baby stopped short. She knew who her first parents were, but didn't know what to do. They knelt down to her level, and she ran to their outstretched arms.

After a morning filled with hugs, kisses and fun, Mom and Dad Hoover said their good-byes and began to walk to their car. Baby watched, then looked up at her adopted mother. Mom Hoover said, "A change had taken place. Baby didn't know whether to go with us, or stay at her new house-but she has made the right decision, and waved goodbye to us." Many visits followed, on a weekly basis. Easter, Christmas, her baptism,-even regular baby-sitting have bound the two families together. Though Baby and her family have relocated since her adoption was finalized, they still live close enough to be reunited on special holidays and on Baby's birthday. Baby is now old enough to write, and she has done so on a regular basis. She still regards the Hoovers as her second set of parents.

Much publicity went out in an attempt to locate Baby's real birth parents, but they were never found. Her story was covered both in newspapers and television. As Mom Hoover sat at the dining room table relating this story to me, tears filled her eyes as she told of giving this dearly beloved child over to her new family. It takes one tough woman to love a child as much as she does, and still be able to hand her over for someone else to rear.

Child abandonment seems to be an increasing social and criminal problem. In 1986, there were an estimated 20,860 abandonments.[3] The Denver-based American Humane Association, which collects such data, said that the number had more than tripled in a decade, and that his figure is probably too low. "It's vastly increased over the last two years," Michael Glenn, a supervisor for Los Angeles County Department of Children's Services said.[4] His department assumes responsibility for abandoned children when they are found. His observation was echoed by many social workers.

Note...

The final chapter entitled "What on Earth is Project Cuddle?" will enlighten you on the exciting answer we have found to this great problem. Until now, people only turned their heads and ignored this horrible issue. Perhaps because there seemed to be no solution. But, as you will see in the pages ahead...there is real hope.

The man behind the woman. Debbe and her husband Dave of over 22 years. Debbe is the founder of a non-profit charity, Project Cuddle, Inc.

Our Carolina Belle with Attorney Julia Tischler who helped Debbe with the first crisis and many others. Julia was instrumental in making this adoption happen.

When the Magnusen family sent out the announcement declaring Elizabeth Dawn and Emily Ann officially had become Magnusens, they sent along this photo!

Emily (above,r) had a mother who had overdosed on cocaine and herion while 6 ½ months pregnant. Though it was only 2 ½ months until the baby was due to be born, her mother still planned to abort her. "I don't want to give birth to a vegetable," she told Dave and Debbe, who picked her up off the street, and helped Emily survive.

Beth and Emily are now in public school and have never visited the principals office except to be praised. They are both happy and healthy. Beth is the singer and thinker. Emily is the comedian and social butterfly.

For Emily, feedings could be quite challenging. She would arch her little back and stiffen her legs; many drug-exposed babies do this, Debbe found.

Tyler in his tuxedo as he arrived at the Magnusen home with Elizabeth, Bejay and Emily.

Our "Belly Button Baby" with his proud and loving mother. Debbe helped instruct over the phone how to make this beautiful little boy's belly button.

Timmy (below) has made much progress since being thrown against the living room wall at two months of age. He now, finally, has a family that loves him!

Debbe is using her bonding techniques on her son Tyler - techniques which have proved invaluable in correcting attachment difficulties.

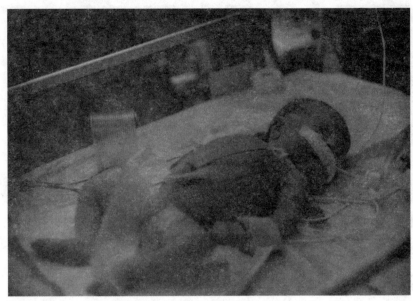

Born exposed to cocaine, heroine and methadone, Emily fought to stay alive. Debbe learned how difficult it would be to forgive Emily's birth mother, but eventually Debbe concluded, "I can honestly now say I love Emmy's mom"-and she does!

The Magnusen Family at Lani & Aaron Scott's wedding. (l to r) Back row: Brian, Lani, Aaron, Bejay,Debbe and Dave. Front row: Emily, Jonathon, Tyler and Elizabeth.

Two of our rescue babies that are now safe in mother's arms.

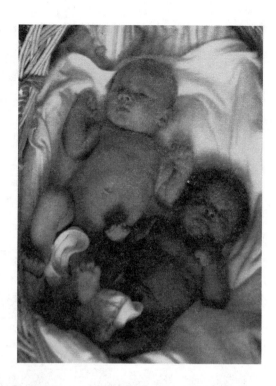

Our "Super Bowl" baby was born on the eve of the Super Bowl in the town where the event was taking place. He is dearly loved by his family.

When Bejay first arrived, the Magnusen's were not given much hope for his future. Words like "institution" and "vegetable" kept coming up...

Through work and bonding techniques developed by the Magnusens, Bejay has turned into a wonderful young man. Bejay is full of life and love, and is one of the most nurturing with the children who have come to their home. Those empty stares have disappeared and he is now attending public school.

Jonathon at seven
months old was
hoping for hair.

Jonathon and his Daddy Dave
all dressed up.

Two Little Indian Boys

The Lintners received a call from Social Services regarding a baby Indian boy, born to an alcoholic mother nearly six months earlier. His birth had been premature, and he had suffered difficulties in swallowing since his birth. Originally he had been sent home with his mother when he was strong enough, but was placed back in the hospital when the visiting nurse discovered the child had not grown, but had actually lost weight. The doctors could not give a very positive outlook for this little boy, who seemed to be nothing more than a vegetable.

Mrs. Lintner told me, "This child was starving to death, due to poor swallowing reflexes and an inattentive mother. He had just wasted away." When she went to the hospital to see him for the first time, she could hardly believe that a child close to his sixth month of life could weigh only eight and a half pounds-the size of a newborn.

The Lintners gave Little Joe that internal drive he so desperately needed to fight for his own survival. She force-fed him, night and day. She was determined that he was not going to die while in her care. After social services observed Little Joe's tremendous progress, they asked the Lintners if they would take in his big brother.

By the time Bobby joined the family, Little Joe had celebrated his first birthday. With his three-year old brother around, Joe was able to attach himself to one more family member. When they had spent three more years with the Lintner family, the boys were told they were to be moved back to the Indian reservation, where they would remain in an Indian foster home until the proper adoptive home could be found. The Lintners asked that they be considered as the adoptive family, but were told that the Indians would not agree to a child from their tribe being adopted by an outsider.

Legal guardianship was then requested by the Lintners, but their request was denied, and they were given only two days to pack all the boys' belongings so they could be transferred to the reservation in South Dakota. The boys both screamed and cried as they were taken by the county workers to a waiting plane.

A week after they had left, Mom Lintner called the social worker to see how the boys were getting along. The woman who had made the decision to return them to the reservation was no longer with the department. They left many messages, but never heard from anyone. After two months had passed, they again contacted the department and explained the whole situation to a new worker. She finally gave them the phone number of the case worker in South Dakota.

The information they received was very distressing. The boys were in the care of their alcoholic grandparents - the same grandparents who lived in a neighboring city while the boys were in the Litner's care, yet never once came to visit during the three years they were in the neighborhood.

After the grandparents were determined to be unfit caregivers, the boys were moved to an Indian foster family, where the father was an officer in the local police department. Not long afterward, they began to suffer the emotional scars of a physically abusive home life. The foster father was evidently beating his wife, especially when he had been drinking too much. It wasn't until the youngest child was hung outside between two trees, suspended by each wrist, stark naked in 32 degree temperature, that the Indian social workers finally removed the boys from this home.

This time they were sent to a home where there was no father at all. The Indian foster mother had three children of her own. They were fairly nice to the boys, but they were treated as outsiders. Whenever the TV was turned on, the boys were told to go to their room. The boys slept in a room with another child, and Little Joe didn't have a bed of his own. He was required to sleep on the floor, and didn't have a blanket to call his own. When the family moved, the boys were relocated with this woman's sister.

The social worker in South Dakota called the Lintners to ask them to write a letter requesting that the boys be reunited with them. She felt the boys had been through so much, they needed a stable home. Very excited, the Lintners complied immediately and had two of their neighbors write letters of reference. It took another year for the social workers to get the details worked out - and six months more before they made the move. The State of California was not anxious to have the children return, and when they did, another six months elapsed before there was any financial aid available to the Lintners.

The morning the boys were to arrive, the Lintners arrived early at the airport. When the big 747 unloaded its cargo, it was an emotional homecoming. Mom Lintner told me, "When we saw each other, we all ran and grabbed one another. The boys clung to us like little monkeys, especially the little one. It took almost a year for him to quit clinging. I knew it was very important, even though inconvenient, for me to stop doing whatever I was doing and just let him run to and cling to me. Now, he's a bit better. He still has to hug and kiss me, like always, when he returns from school, or from visiting a friend."

The older boy asked if the yellow wading pool was still at the house-the one he remembered before he had been taken away. His Mom told him that everything was still the same - and that it would stay that way, just as their relationship would...

Update...

Bobby and Little Joe have now been with the Lintners for over five years, and both have been legally adopted. The boys are doing well in school, but they are still trying to deal emotionally with all the hardship they endured.

We all need to remember to stand up for children's rights, to press on in the children's best interest. Some social workers do not always make correct decisions, though most are conscientious and make good decisions.

As our interview ended, I had the pleasure of meeting both of these wonderful young boys. Any parent would be proud to have the honor of rearing them. Fortunately, Mom and Dad Lintner have that honor!

The Thompson Children

"Guilty," the jury foreman read. "Guilty on all counts." Samuel Thompson looked off into space. There was no change of expression-he didn't even flinch.

The courtroom buzzed with definite pleasure at the news. "Thank God," one woman yelled in the back of the courtroom.

The young man sitting at the prosecutor's table leaned back in his chair as the decision was read. Tears welled up in his eyes; he tried to blink them away. This verdict would never make up for all he and his brothers had suffered, but at least it would make his father pay for what he had done.

As the hand-cuffed Mr. Thompson was taken away through the court chambers, his son walked silently through the main court room entrance. The press, anxious for a story, lunged at him with questions about his feelings regarding the verdict.

"I'm sorry, but Jesse is not answering any questions at this time," the attorney said as he escorted his client down the courthouse steps. The news media persisted until Jesse and his attorney got into the waiting car, which pulled away from the curb.

Joan had been following the case for many years. As I spoke with her, she began to talk about how she got involved. "It was a long time ago, but I remember getting a call from a social worker asking if we would be willing to take in a six year old boy. I didn't realize at the time what this little boy had gone through, but after meeting him for lunch, we decided to give him a try in our home. I remember he arrived wearing a pair of men's underwear. That little boy had all his belongings in the world in one bag: a T-shirt, a pair of men's underwear, and a pair of socks. At six years of age, that's all he owned!"

"This child started life in Hell," Joan continued as she filled me in on details of his case. Tony was dangled by his heels out a four-story window - as were his brothers - when their father wanted their mother to perform sexually. Still, the children remained in this insane environment until one day when Tony's big brother, thirteen-year old Jesse, lay dying on the kitchen table. Tony came home from school to find the most horrifying sight possible. Their father had gotten angry at Jesse for not performing a sexual act as well as he was expected, and in a rage their father cut off Jesse's penis with a pocket knife.

Hysterically, Tony ran down the hallway of the apartment complex, where he was able to get help for Jesse, who came close to bleeding to death. This scene was engraved on Tony's mind when he entered Joan and Jim's home. At least twice a night they would listen to

73

his blood-curdling screams, because of his horrible nightmares. The bed wetting occurred just as frequently.

"Tony was a lot like a jawbreaker, I heard Joan say. "We had the usual honeymoon period, but he wasn't about to let any woman come into his world. He had seen how his mother allowed all those horrible things to happen to his brothers and to himself, and because of this he couldn't bring himself to respect a woman. He was extremely angry at the only woman he knew, because she never stood up for the boys and their safety."

"It was really hard, because he wouldn't allow me to get close. Jim could talk to him, but he didn't want anything to do with me," Joan continued. Six months passed after Tony's arrival, and he was anxious to see his younger brother, Mark. It seemed like a good idea, since the nightmares were diminishing to one per night. He loved his little brother, and constantly asked about him. The meeting was arranged, and it seemed to go fairly well at first, but as this visit progressed it became apparent that it was too difficult for Tony to handle. Too many horrible memories returned, and Tony regressed in his therapy. This unfortunate setback made those in charge of Tony's case realize that even though there was a lot of love between the boys, it was not in Tony's best interest for the association to continue.

Tony stayed with Jim and Joan for a year and a half. By the time he left, he had softened to the point that he could give her a hug-but still he held most of his thoughts wrapped tightly around his heart. Joan felt she at least had a chance to show this young man that, through her determination and love, at least some women are worthy of being trusted.

Update...

Jesse joined the Navy, and is doing quite well. When he turned 21, he came back on temporary leave in order to press charges against his father. (This can only be done when a person becomes an adult.) The youngest brother, Mark, was adopted by a wonderful family, and is doing fine. Tony was placed in an adoptive home, but that adoption failed. Since then, he has been placed in a home with a family of five children, and is now doing wonderfully. For a child that "started life by living in Hell," he has done well...

Mommy, What's a Hooker?

Christine's Story

November 12th: I received a phone call from Christine, mother of Billy Joe. I had heard from her only one other time, during the six months Billy Joe had been in our care as a foster child. On that occasion, Christine called to set up a visitation for Billy's third birthday-but she never showed up. Every time Billy Joe was asked to draw a picture of his mother, he would draw a circle with nothing in it. I wanted him to see her again so that he would have something to draw in that circle. I have learned over the years not to let a child know when a parent is planning to come-it can be such a let-down if the parent doesn't arrive.

"Bud locked me out of my hotel room last night, and all I have on is my baby doll nightie. I don't even have a pair of shoes. Please, can you bring me something? It's so cold," Christine complained.

Billy and his sister, Candice, had been removed from their mother's care when she was found unconscious with a syringe on the floor beside her. There were no clean clothes in the house, and no food. Both Billy and his sister didn't think things were so bad; after all, that was what they were used to. The children had dealt with not only physical neglect, but also they endured mental abuse. Bud, his mother's pimp, used to hold a knife up to Christine's neck, then say, "Come here and watch, kids, while I stab your mother..."

We asked if we could bring Billy along in order to see her. At first Christine told us no, because she didn't want him to see her like this. I explained how Billy had no memories of what she looked like and how he had talked of seeing her. She finally agreed that it might be the best thing for her son and told us where to meet.

We found Christine, living with one of her "clients." It was hard to imagine, with her belly so swollen, she was still planning on aborting the baby. We pleaded with her not to kill the precious little child she was carrying. We promised to become its foster parents or adopt, whichever she wanted. Christine was barely five feet tall. One of her side teeth had been broken off, and the gap could be seen as she smiled at her little boy for the first time in six months. "Come here, Billy Joe," she cheerfully commanded, and Billy walked sheepishly toward her, never allowing their eyes to meet. Christine talked to us as she put on some of the clothes we brought. Billy watched silently. I wondered what he was thinking.

It was a relief to leave the apartment which was decorated with Playboy and comparable pin ups; I decided we had all had enough education for one day. At the nearest hamburger joint Christine allowed us to buy her only a large coke. While she drank it, she talked with Billy as he bounced from booth to the floor and back - loving every minute of this time with his mother. It was good for him to be able to put a face in his drawing.

Finishing our sandwiches, we took photos of Billy Joe and his mother, then drove back to the dingy apartment, where we let her out. We could only pray that we would see her again: the Lord willing, we would.

November 23rd: I received a phone call from Bud. "I think you'd better get Christine. I saw her on a street corner and she's in a bad way. There's something wrong. I'm really worried about her, but I don't know who else to call." I asked him how he got this number and he told me that he had found it hidden in her bra when she was unconsious right before the broke up.

I told Bud we'd get help to Christine right away and within minutes my husband, Dave, was in his little sports car, heading toward the grungy motel that served as home for Christine and her baby. When Dave returned, Christine's cigarette-smoke-filled clothes combined with cheap perfume made a nauseating blend. Dave's poor car would never be the same. "I'll be glad for you to have the baby," she told us, "since you already have Billy." What about Bud, we wondered. "Oh, Bud says just get rid of it, it's not his baby anyway. 'Just get rid of the damn thing,' he said..." Christine's voice trailed off, and she dramatically announced, "Oh, gee, I'm really in labor!"

Because of the lack of prenatal care, we had no idea how far along she actually was. For all we knew, at this point, we were about to greet the newest arrival to our home. I told her that it would be best to get to the hospital in case she was about to deliver. She told me she didin't want to go. I eventually made a deal with her. She would go to the hospital on one condition...that I would buy her a baked potato at Carl's Jr. with extra everything on it. By the time I left the drive-thru and drove the five miles to the hospital, she had inhaled the entire thing.

As we arrived at this upper crust hospital, they seemed a bit shocked, yet receptive to helping us with this young woman. We told the woman at the emergency room desk that we thought Christine was due to deliver any minute and was currently in labor.How wrong we were! Tests made at the hospital showed the baby still needed two and a half months of time to grow. They got Christine upstairs and hooked up to the fetal monitor. She had fallen into an incoherent state. I approached her bedside and asked a question, but received no response that made sense.

The head nurse motioned me to step into the hallway. "This is very typical of how a person reacts after an overdose. When they are 'coming down,' they'll sleep like this for hours." What was she talking about? The nurse leaned closer to me. "She overdosed on heroin and cocaine! We have her stabilized now, and you will need to transfer her to another hospital," the nurse sympathetically advised me.

I pulled my car up to the ambulance entrance and laid back the passenger seat as far as it would go. Christine barely moved as the nurses helped relocate her from the gurney to the car.

The baby was in fetal distress and Christine would need someone to sit with her for the next twelve hours, I was told. I explained to the staff that I had five children at home and had been sick with 104 degree fever myself. But there was no one else. If Christine got up and got hold of more drugs, she and the baby would die. So, all night long I sat beside her and listened to the heart beat of Christine's little baby. When the repetitious beats would slow down or falter, I would quickly pray for that little heart to start regular beating again. I fell in love with that baby during those quiet hours at the hospital.

Next morning before I left, Christine awakened and groggily told me she wanted to clean up her act and get off drugs. She also told me she had asked to be tested for HIV and AIDS antibodies, and had asked that the test results be given to me. The main goal of the next few weeks was to keep her from "working" on the streets. The doctor explained to us that it was extremely important for Christine to either get on a Methadone program, or if this was not possible, to let her use only enough drugs to avoid severe withdrawal. At all costs, we were to try to get her to avoid premature labor.[5]

Back at home I called every drug program, every rehabilitation center around. Between 50 and 70 calls were made that day, from Riverside to San Diego counties. No one wanted a seven-month pregnant prostitute going through withdrawal. Experts, I knew, don't advise detoxification, due to the fact that it might provoke pre-term labor or fetal distress.[6] Christine really had no place to go when she was released from the hospital except back to the man she had been with prior to overdosing. We knew that there was a warrant outstanding for her arrest for prostitution, so my prayer partner and I began to pray that she would be picked up and placed on a Methadone program in jail...

December 15th: Christine decided to take a bus to find her old pimp. The fellow she has been staying with after Bud threw her out was against this, but said he would accompany her to Bud's place. Somehow, Christine and her gentleman friend got into an argument on the bus, and the bus driver finally asked them to get off. As Christine started down the steps, her companion called out her name. She turned toward him, and he swung his umbrella at her face. This was no ordinary umbrella: a machete was concealed inside. As she leaped toward the street curb, he continued to swing wildly. Christine did not see the parking sign sticking up from the asphalt directly in front of her, and she hit the sturdy sign, tumbled to the ground and fell flat on her swollen belly. Police were called to the scene and began to ask questions of the victim and her assailant.

Usually, Christine used a fictitious name when being questioned by the police, but this time she told them the truth. The officer noted the warrant outstanding for her arrest, and took her to the O.B. ward at the hospital, with an officer posted outside her door at all times. She called to let us know what had happened, and also to let us know they had started her on the Methadone program. She had been in premature labor again, but was now stable, and would probably remain there for four or five days, after which she would be transferred to the jail infirmary. Our prayers were answered!

February 2nd: The phone call finally came that Christine was in labor. I raced to the hospital and impatiently waited while the elevator doors opened and closed without a sign of her. Finally, the doors opened again-leaving no doubt that Christine was arriving. Surrounding her gurney were three sheriffs in complete uniform including guns, two ambulance attendants, and a very attractive female deputy. This parade of people made quite a scene as they walked down the hallway enroute to the examining area. The five men came back out after five minutes, and one of them told me to have a seat and that I would hear from the remaining sheriff in a bit.

Much to my amazement, Christine and her guard came out of the examining room together. Christine was still wearing the bright orange, one-piece jumpsuit in which she had arrived. Christine said, "They want me to walk because I'm only dilated to three. Why don't you come and walk with us?"

Since I was reared in the quiet and proper city of Newport Beach, California this was all very foreign to me. I knew that all eyes were on us as I followed behind the very pregnant women who advertised "O.C. Jail" on the front and back of her bright orange prison garb. I knew that in the next few hours a decision would have to be made by Christine as to whether or not we were going to be adopting or fostering her new child. This wasn't going to be an easy decision for Christine. I also knew that I had to accept with my heart the decision that was made. I had already been informed that I shouldn't have gotten as close to this situation as I had. But if I hadn't listened with my heart, there might have been no baby and no Christine: they might have died back in November. No, I knew that what I was doing was what God wanted me to be doing; I felt secure in my decisions.

When Christine returned for another examination, I decided to go to the cafeteria. I was assured there was plenty of time to enjoy a little lunch before anything happened. On my way back to the labor room, I started to get excited over being Christine's coach. But neither Christine nor her sheriff were anywhere to be found. Just then the double doors burst open, and the deputy had a big smile on her face. "It's here, it's here!"

I stopped dead in my tracks. "It's a girl! She was born in the labor room. The doctors are working on the baby now, but Christine is doing fine." What a relief! But I was unaware that at that moment the little five-pound girl was fighting for her life in the room just behind me. She had inhaled the meconium (her first bowel movement) and would have to be put on life support.[7]

I followed the incubator into ICU, where I met the doctor. "Well," he said, then sighed. "She'd sure have a lot better chance of surviving if she had more weight on her." Suddenly my blood began to boil. I had just heard Christine say how much she loved this little baby. Now I discovered that her selfish indulgences, not only with drugs, but with her wasting money on candy and cokes as she sat in jail might cost this innocent little baby her life. It was beyond me!

That's when I asked for God's help. Sure enough, He came through, as He always does. When I listened with my heart, I was able to see that even though Jesus was being hung on the cross, He still loved the people who were hanging Him. Sure, He didn't love what they were doing, but He loved them. Somehow, I had to feel the same way toward Christine. I had to forgive her. Now, I can honestly say, "I love Christine and I always will." She was hurting from things I will never fully understand. I needed to help her by praying for her.

It wasn't until Christine signed the birth certificate that we became aware of the fact that she had chosen "Emily"-my girl friend's name that we had picked when adoption had been discussed. When Emily was ready to be released, we were asked to sign the papers giving us permission to care for her and to seek council for private adoption. This was done at Christine's request. Dave and I had talked it over, and we both felt uncomfortable about doing anything without Social Services being involved. If Christine decided when she got out of jail that she would just come and pick up Emily, we would have no recourse. So instead of signing the papers that Emily be released to us, we refused. This immediately put a police hold on Emily-because this means the baby had been abandoned. With no one to pick her up. Social Services must come to the rescue, and Emily had to be taken to the Children's Home. Emily was to stay there until the hearing, to be held two days later.

February 5th: ALL things work together for good, to them that love the Lord and are called according to His purpose. Christine's oldest child, Candice, was living in the Children's Home. Unless Emily had been sent there Candice would never have been allowed to see her baby sister. "Is she really my sister?" Candice wanted to know. " She doesn't really look like me, does she?"-and we realized Candice really wanted to hear that she did. "Oh, yes, Candice, she really does. Just look at those beautiful big eyes, just like yours. Do you want to hold her?" "Could I? Sure! I'd love to," Candice beamed. She cradled the baby close to her, rocking back and forth. Then we took Emily into our hearts and home. We pray for her and love her, knowing her stay with us will be as long as God desires. We know that God's perfect timing is best!

Update...

Candice moved back to Virginia to be with her father. She is doing quite well. Christine was re-arrested and ordered to attend a drug rehabilitation program. She has since accepted the Lord as her personal Savior, she is due to get out of prison in a few months. Presently, she is clean, and hoping to stay that way.

And Emily...well, she is now a Magnusen. We finished our adoption in May, 1991-and for this, we are very happy. We can't imagine life without our little Emily. She will serve as a constant reminder to us as to why we should listen to God, and to remember that sometimes He leads us through our hearts...

And There's Still More...

The Martinez Family

The reason behind this chapter heading is very simple: the children we see now coming into "the system" have changed. Social Services used to receive children from under-privileged homes, or children who were orphaned. Now all this has changed. Today we are seeing cases which can usually be linked in some way to the drug problems of our country. Whether it's a prostitute who's been arrested, who needs shelter for her child while serving time-or whether it's a pusher who is abusing his "old lady's kids," the abuse and neglect of children today point toward drug abuse.

The majority of foster mothers get upset about the fact that there is an extremely high percentage of these women who have not one or two, but sometimes MANY children, all of whom are then placed in the foster care system. I would like to introduce you to one of these women, and give you an example involving our family, personally.

Though the child involved came into our care only four and a half years ago, her family had been a client of Social Services for the past seven years. It started in 1983. Juanita and her husband, Carlos, lived in a very nice home on the outskirts of Santa Barbara. They had three children: Maria, six, Franco who was three, and the youngest child, Victor, barely a year old.

Everything was going just fine for this quiet little family. Carlos had just received a raise, and Juanita was busy fixing up their first house, making it into a real home. Maria was doing fine in first grade, and Franco enjoyed playing with his little brother. How quickly the rug was pulled out from under this sweet young couple.

That Monday started out like every other Monday. Juanita had gotten up early, made lunches for Maria and Carlos, and kissed them goodbye. She went back into the house to start straightening things up. Juanita had placed Franco and Victor in front of the television, then started loading the dishes into the dishwasher. She had left the boys in the other room for only five minutes when she decided things were too quiet, and she had better go check on them. Victor was staring glassy-eyed at the TV, but Franco was nowhere to be found. Juanita looked under the beds, hoping he was just playing a game. He didn't come out when she called to him, so she went into the garage to see if he was perhaps playing with Grandpa's tools. Still, no Franco.

Juanita felt her stomach begin to flutter with apprehension. She knew she had closed the gate leading to the pool, but just to be safe, she decided to check. Juanita ran through the garage, toward the back yard. Her gut feeling was that Franco was in the pool. She had tried to talk Carlos out of buying that house for that very reason. She would never forgive him if something happened to Franco.

As she opened the back door, she saw the gate was ajar. Yelling for Franco, she felt her heart stop when she saw his limp body floating in the far end of the pool. She screamed at the top of her lungs, "My baby! My baby! Someone help me, please!" As she leaned over the edge of the pool, a neighbor who had heard all the commotion peeked over the fence. "Hang on, honey, I'll call for help," she told Juanita. After placing the call to 9-1-1 she scaled the fence and jumped in the pool, scooping up the child in one deft maneuver. She handed the limp body to Juanita.

The sirens wailed at Juanita's home, and her neighbor climbed out of the pool and raced toward the blaring sounds out front. She wanted to make sure help came to the right house, though deep down she had a feeling it was too late for Franco. "Through here! Hurry! He's in bad shape-just go right on out in back!" the neighbor told the paramedics. She began to shake as she made her way back to Juanita's side.

What speed they used while trying to revive Franco! The paramedics decided not to wait for an ambulance, but instead carried Franco in the cab of their emergency vehicle and raced right to the hospital. Franco didn't make it. He was declared dead on arrival. They had to sedate Juanita, because the shock was so great. This was to prove a turning point for the whole Martinez family.

Juanita carried the guilt of Franco's death with her in years to come. She never recovered from this tragedy, and in fact ended up doing things she never thought imaginable. By the time Maria was 12, she had been abandoned by her mother four different times. Juanita had become part of the "cocaine scene," and was unable to think clearly about her children's needs.

Sometimes when she was on drugs she would be gone for days at a time-then Maria would be in charge. Carlos left his wife a year to the day after their son's death. He was never forgiven by Juanita, and felt their constant arguing wasn't good for the children. The final shove came when Carlos saw that Juanita was "shooting up" in their dining room.

Shortly after Carlos left, Juanita found herself pregnant with child number four. This little one would suffer the effects of alcohol, heroin and cocaine upon its birth. Juanita did not seek any medical care, and had no idea when she would be due. She figured she had already given birth to enough of them that she really didn't need medical care. Besides, she thought, "What would they do if they found out I am 'using'?"

And There's Still More...

So her pregnancy progressed until she shot up one too many times. Her belly twisted into knots that sent her into such pain she wished she was dead. Someone at the party offered to drop her off at the hospital, as long as they wouldn't have to give their name. Juanita hitched her donated ride to the hospital and was quickly wheeled into the examining room. When the nurse took one look at Juanita's arms, she knew this lady was in trouble. She stared at the bulging lumps that once were called veins. Some marks were fresh, others black and blue from repeated attempts to get that needle in. At least two different spots were abscessed, and probably had been for some time.

Juanita looked away as the nurse did her inspection. She knew what the woman must be thinking, and she wasn't feeling up to a lecture. "Look, you and I both know what caused this, and I want the truth for your medical history. We're going to need it for the baby's sake," the nurse said with a snap in her voice.

"I know, I know, just give me something for the pain. I'll tell you anything you want to know. This pain is horrible," Juanita whined, as she tossed from side to side. The doctor was summoned, tests ordered, and they confirmed his suspicions: the baby was in fetal distress, and was about 34 weeks along. The decision was made to take the baby by Cesarean section. Within fifteen minutes of entering the O.R., the doctor announced, "It's a boy!" The tiny, squalling newborn was quickly suctioned and handed to the waiting pediatrician. After a quick examination, he was placed into the waiting incubator, then transferred to ICU.

After a good night's rest, the social worker came in to visit with Juanita. She explained that they had found traces of alcohol, heroin and cocaine in the baby's system, and that there was the possibility that her son would be removed from her care. But after further investigation, Social Services decided to allow her to take her child home with her. After all, this had never happened to Juanita before. The two children she had at home seemed to be doing just fine, so they dropped the case on this little one.

Juanita decided to name her little boy after the son she had lost. She hoped God was replacing dear Franco in this baby's body. So she gave herself the last of the cocaine she had smuggled into the hospital, then signed out Franco Raul Martinez and herself. She was sure that with Franco II in her life, she would be able to make a clean start. Things would be different this time, she told everyone who would listen...

By the time Franco II was two, he was about to become a big

brother. Since Maria was now ten, she was in charge of cooking all the meals, and also did diapers for Franco. She didn't mind-it made her feel important.

Pregnant again, Juanita was selling herself on street corners. She tried to wear clothes that hid her swollen condition. It wasn't easy being pregnant and trying to look sexy enough to get picked up. But somehow she had to bring in some money. Her next fix had to be paid for, or she and the baby would both suffer from drug withdrawal.

Juanita hit it big this time - she earned double her normal fee, just because the guy was in a good mood. She decided to celebrate with her girl friend, Casey - who worked the same corner. Anxiously they paged their drug dealer, and waited for him at the corner liquor store. After making the transaction, they returned to Casey's place. This was gonna be one BIG party, they thought...

Within five minutes of shooting up, Juanita knew she was in trouble. Something was wrong with the baby, and she knew she'd better get to the hospital. By the time she got a taxi to stop, she was feeling faint. "Please hurry, sir," she wearily pleaded as the driver did his best to dodge traffic. "Hang in there, lady, we're almost there," he nervously told Juanita. Rounding the drive to the Emergency entrance, the cabby slammed the car into park, jumped out to summon a passing attendant and within moments Juanita was surrounded by medical personnel.

A preliminary ultrasound revealed not one baby in distress, but two! They had to operate..NOW! Pandemonium broke loose as the medical staff prepared for this emergency. The first to be born, a little boy weighing 3 pounds, 2 ounces, was later named Geraldo Saul. Two minutes afterward, Beth Olivia was delivered-but she weighed only 2 pounds, 6 ounces. The doctors estimated they were nearly three months premature. Both babies were jittering uncontrollably and needed oxygen immediately. When Juanita recovered, she was told that it would be touch and go for the next few weeks.

Geraldo began to respond to treatment, but Beth did not do well. The doctors had to perform an emergency operation on her fragile little heart to correct a defect. On the third day of life, Beth's frail and exhausted body gave up. For three days she had been subjected to a living Hell. This was an experience no child deserved, but she had to go through it, and go through it alone.

One would think that after giving birth to three babies born exposed to cocaine and alcohol, a lesson would have been learned. WRONG!!! Juanita lost custody of Geraldo, watched Beth die, watched Franco II struggle to speak normally, and yet she was pregnant again within three months. During her seventh pregnancy, social services received a distressing call from a woman claiming to be the baby-sitter for Maria and Franco II Martinez. She told officials that Juanita had left the children with her for almost a month, and that she just couldn't keep them any longer. She had no idea where their mother was to be found.

Maria knew the routine, and courteously followed the police officer over to the patrol unit. She knew that he would take her to the home with other children. Franco II was only three, and he didn't understand why he was being arrested again.

No one heard from Juanita until the ambulance transported her from the dingy motel room to the county trauma center. When the medical staff retrieved her records, they knew they had better get ready to call in a social worker as soon as the baby was born. They could only hope this child fared better than the last two. Another C-section, and Juanita was presented with another daughter. She chose to name this child after the daughter she would never see again. Her name: Beth Olivia Martinez II. She weighed 4 pounds, 8 ounces and was born six weeks prematurely. She was more beautiful than any of the other children, and Juanita prayed that she would be able to clean herself up this time.

Beth was very petite, and would require lots of TLC We first saw her when she was two months old. I took care of her one day when her foster mother wanted to take her other children to the fair. It turned out to be a pleasant afternoon, and by the time Beth was ready to leave, Dave and I had begun to ask each other if we should consider taking her on a full-time basis.

After much prayer, we all went to bed, planning to take a family vote in the morning. During the night, I had a dream. In my dream, Beth was our baby and we were celebrating Easter Day. I remember vividly tossing her up in the air, watching her dark curls bounce up and down. When I awoke, I knew that Beth was destined to be in our home.

One month and many papers later, Beth was placed in our care. She and Bejay are only six months apart in age, so they think of themselves as twins. She has very fine features, but makes up for the appearance of daintiness with iron-willed determination. Someday this will benefit her and she will make it in whatever she chooses.

Update...

Since Beth was placed with us, her mother delivered her eighth child. Since she is now only 28 years of age, it will probably not be her last. Maria ran away from a wonderful foster home to join one of the local gangs. Victor and Franco II are back in the custody of their mother. Geraldo was placed in a foster home for high risk children, and the parents have since decided to adopt. He is still on oxygen and many medications, but is progressing. We adopted Beth, and when it was finalized, her announcement read: "I may be little and mighty, but now I'm a Magnusen too!"

Note...

There are hundreds and possibly thousands of drug-dependent women who are repeatedly giving birth to drug-exposed baby after drug-exposed baby. Nothing has a higher priority for them than getting that next fix. Unless new programs are available to those that are pregnant, and more education provided to help in caring for these babies we're all going to suffer in years to come. These child victims may become tomorrow's criminals.

I don't intend to scare anyone, but simply to increase awareness. It has to become everyone's responsibility to help protect our families' futures. If we don't...who will?

Timothy's Story

For the previous eighteen years, Nancy and Charles Miller had cared for abused and neglected children. They cringed whenever the details of a new, tragic case were explained to them, but when they heard Timmy's story, it twisted knots in their stomachs...

Timmy had been born on a crisp October day, as the rest of the world watched the fall leaves turn shades of red, amber and gold. The delivery had gone smoothly, and no real complications seemed to be in store for Kelly Korder and her new son.

She had been hoping for a little boy she could name after her latest boyfriend, the father of her child. So Kelly was in luck. She named him Timothy Fabian and planned to call him Jr. She reasoned that if she showed her boyfriend how important he was to her by using his name, he might be willing to marry her at last. She had already given birth to three little girls by the same man, and hoped he would see things differently once a son was born.

As Kelly sat up in her hospital bed, she peered over the edge of his little incubator. She had such plans for this one. He would do all the things his Dad had missed. He could complete high school and she would make sure that he would become the first in the family to go on to college. This was going to be a child to make everyone proud.

Unfortunately, Kelly wasn't going to get the privilege of seeing her beautiful boy grow up-and it almost turned out that no one else would, either. The social worker began to unfold the details of Timmy's brief life to Nancy and Charles. She told them that Kelly and her mother apparently got into an argument over something Kelly had forgotten. Kelly was determined to win this battle, and she didn't care what the price would be - she knew she was right, and that was that. She became more and more out of control as the argument escalated, and began throwing shoes piled in a laundry basket beside her. Kelly's mother ran for the kitchen to escape any more abuse. As she rounded the corner and leaned against the kitchen counter, she heard a noise like none she had ever heard before. It was a loud "thump," and plates on the wall shook.

"You're crazy," the old woman shouted, as she picked up her purse from the kitchen table. "I've had enough of this-I'm leaving'. Stop that baby's crying, Kelly," she ordered as she slipped out the back door and down the steps.

What Timmy's grandmother didn't know was that her grandson's whole life had been seriously changed in that last few minutes. He would never be the same again. Blood-curdling screams penetrated the thin walls of Kelly's house for the next day. Timmy was about to have his first Christmas, but this wasn't the way things were supposed to be. Kelly turned the stereo up to block out that obnoxious scream-ing. The tiny two-month old, finally quieted down that first night. On the second day, he was silent.

Kelly's mother returned to visit after taking two days respite, away from Kelly and her terrible temper. She hoped that Kelly had cooled down enough so they could pick up the splintered pieces of their rela-tionship, as they had so many other times. Kelly's mom carried an arm-ful of Christmas gifts as she climbed the steps to the front door of the house. She hadn't even reached the final step when Kelly's oldest daugh-ter, Tiffany, swung open the old wooden screen and said, "Hi, Grandma. What'cha got for me?" Tiffany's two little sisters - Tally, age 4 and Tasha, 3 followed their big sister's lead, as they ran to investigate the gift cards on each package.

"Now wait a second, girls. These go under the Christmas tree. We have to wait until after we have that turkey dinner. Here, you kids can help me put them in the perfect spot," she said. As the girls entered the living room, their grandmother followed behind, but stopped dead in her tracks. She couldn't believe the state of that room. Kelly was nowhere to be seen. Shoes still lay on the floor where they had landed two days earlier. Beer bottles, cigarettes and dirty paper plates cov-ered everything. In the far corner of the room lay a dirty old towel, that moved just a bit. Someone was under that lump.

While the girls began to relieve their grandmother of her heavy load, she said: "What'cha doin' over there, Timmy? Here, punkin' let's come look at the presents." A terrible smell offended her senses, as she approached the bundle. She thought to herself, there was no way this putrid odor could come from little Timmy. The closer she drew to his cold, damp resting place the more she realized the smell WAS coming from Timmy. She tried to block out the reality of what she saw...

It was as though a person had taken off the most beautiful bud from a rose bush, then stepped on it and left it to die. Timmy's face was pale against the bright Christmas lights. He lay expressionless as she began to remove the towel. The little girls were ever so busy repo-sitioning their gifts, and had no clue of the terror growing in their grandmother's heart. Suddenly, the background sounds of holiday songs were drowned out by the ear-splitting screams of Timmy's grandmother. "Quick, dial 9-1-1! Oh, God, don't let him die!" she wailed. She desper-ately wanted to hold him to her breast, but she knew he must not be moved. The five minutes the paramedics took to get there seemed like five hours.

The three little girls had been ordered to stand out front and flag down the paramedic's truck. They weren't sure what had happened inside the living room, but they knew it must be pretty bad to upset their grandma so. They bounced up and down as they heard the approaching shrill sound of the sirens. Their laughter broke into exhilarated cheers as they saw the red and white lights flashing against the side of the house. They were totally unaware that their little brother was the cause of all this excitement, with his very life hanging in the balance.

The paramedics leaped from their truck, retrieved their gear, and ran toward the front door, where they could see a woman in her late 50's pacing back and forth in front of a little mound. When they reached for the screen door, they heard the woman's distressed sobs - and knew they had the right place. She was so distraught, she didn't even hear one medic speaking to her as he gently touched her on the shoulder, then guided her to the sofa, where he again asked her for any information she could give.

The other medic set his medical box down, then carefully opened it up. Before investigating the victim, he wanted everything laid out and available. He gently raised the towel from the tiny patient, and momentarily froze. "Come here, Scott, NOW!" His tone was calm, yet firm.

What lay before them was the worst case of child abuse they had ever seen, or ever hoped to see. One arm lay above the baby's head, black and blue from the tip of the fingers to the top of the shoulder. It had swollen to double its normal size, and obviously was in need of immediate medical help. On closer examination, they discovered he had a shattered pelvic bone, and many other injuries.

"Call Greenbrook General, tell them we have MAJOR injuries coming in," Scott was told. By the time the ambulance took off with little Timmy, the child had already gone into cardiac arrest once, and was at risk for having it happen again. The ER personnel anxiously awaited their newest patient, and had propped open the electric doors, to save time for his entrance. An orthopedic surgeon, a neurologist, and an internist had been summoned. "Code white in the ER Code white," they heard over the loud speaker. This meant an emergency involving life or death, and the victim is a child. As the gurney whisked through the ER lobby and into the trauma room, lights switched on and an X-ray machine was quickly wheeled into place. It was hours before all the tests had been completed. While they worked, every staff member tensed up as they heard the raving cries of a woman entering the ER "Where's my baby? I want my baby!"

One of the doctors whispered something to the nurse at his side, who disappeared into the main lobby. She walked directly over to the security guard, and within moments, city patrol units were at the ER door. Gently but firmly, Kelly was escorted to a small side room.

At first, she denied doing such a horrible thing. She told them the baby had fallen off the changing table while she had gone to the phone. The story then changed to a stranger whom she claimed entered the house and hit her baby because she would not give him money. Finally, after hours of exhausting all other believable avenues for getting off the hook, Kelly told them the truth.

With not a tear in her eyes Kelly related the details of Timmy's injuries. Her statement raised the hairs on the back of the officers' necks. "I was so mad at my mom, that I started throwing shoes. I ran out of shoes, and so I threw Timmy..."

After spending two months in the hospital for a fractured skull, hemorrhaging in the brain that led to permanent blindness, his broken arms, broken pelvis, broken ribs, and fractured leg were beginning to mend. Timmy was transferred to a board and care facility that cared for children on a short-term basis.

Their work was really cut out for them at Social Services. They were going to have a difficult time finding someone willing to take a child with all the handicaps Timmy had. It was getting more and more difficult to find good homes for "normal" kids, let alone ones with special needs. Fortunately for everyone involved, they had heard the Miller family had a vacancy, and since Nancy was a registered nurse, she would be a great one to help this frail, mending 5-month old baby.

When Nancy and Charles first laid eyes on him, they knew little Timmy belonged in their home. Arrangements were made with Social Services, while the Millers went busily to work getting out the old crib which had held so many before him. The whole family drove along to welcome him, and he was lifted into the car with casts on his legs and arms.

The first two months he was with them Timmy refused to allow the Millers to cuddle him. He made absolutely NO sound-any sound-to let them know he was trying to fight to live. Finally, on the Fourth of July, real fireworks broke loose at the Millers! As Nancy lowered him into his highchair he tipped over to one side. He was so startled, he let out a real scream for the first time! Nancy still remembers that moment, and declares, "It was the best sound we had ever heard!"

After that day, Timmy allowed himself to start feeling, and allowed the Millers to love him in return. He got especially close to Charles, and would wriggle with excitement when he heard his foster Dad approaching. For reasons only God knows, Charles' time came to meet the Lord in Heaven. When I asked Nancy how she could handle Timmy with all the responsibilities she was carrying, she told me, "I didn't have time to think about what had happened. I was shaken by Charles' death, but knew I had to carry on. Sometimes I think about other widows and wonder, what do they do with themselves? How do they pass their time? Then I return to caring for my little ones."

Update...

Nancy has now adopted Timmy, and says that he is the best natured child. He can't walk, and is blind, as well as developmentally delayed, but loved very much.

Kelly was found guilty of child abuse, and is now serving time in jail. She saw Timmy only once, after that fateful night, and that was when she said her final good-bye to him. She was more concerned with whether or not the other prisoners had seen Timmy, than with how he was doing. She knew prisoners would be "roughed up" if they had hurt a child. After spending an hour with Timmy, she got up and walked towards the door. She stopped, turned, and waved to the son she was giving up, and somehow at that very moment he waved his little hand in the air. Since he is totally blind, we'll never know what caused him to make that gesture, but it made Kelly feel a little better, and made Nancy chuckle inside.

Kelly's live-in boyfriend was also charged with child abuse because he didn't seek the medical help Timmy so desperately needed. We will never know how he and Kelly could have allowed that broken, pathetic baby to lie in his own excrement for two whole days, with all those broken bones-but Nancy Miller and Master Timothy Miller are so very thankful that he was finally found...

Our Own Little Tigger & Pooh

Okay, we really thought that we were to finish our family with 2 "original models" (those we made) and three adopted children. However, the best laid plans at the Magnusen home often lead to adoption. So, we now have two more wonderful children that will permanently be a part of our lives. Let me introduce you to them and their stories.

Our Little Tigger

Winter was in full force and Paula was really getting in the mood to celebrate the Christmas season. She began calling everyone she knew and inviting them over to her place. The apartment wasn't very big, but the neighbors wouldn't complain about the noise or their using the courtyard area as long as you gave each one a six-pack of beer. Red and green streamers hung from the dining room chandelier and Paula now turned her efforts towards filling some large, white, plastic trash bags with newspaper. There may not be snow in most of Southern California, but there she could still make a mean looking snowman out of these trash bags. Kenny was Paula's oldest son. He was a very handsome little boy, with beautiful blonde hair. He walked into the living room. "What are you doing mom?" Kenny asked Paula. She anxiously answered Kenny as she lifted the third and final bag up onto the snowman's body. "We're having a party mi hijo". (mi hijo is Spanish for my son) "Cool" remarked the seven year old. He always loved the way mom had parties. The best part to him was when people would get drunk and fall down, or say things that didn't make sense in Spanish or English. Yep, he was going to have a good night. As the sun began to set, the guests began to arrive. Most of Paula's friends brought their own booze, along with their own drug or drugs of choice. Everybody shared, after all they were "friends". The kitchen counter had two pyramids of cans. The first was those that were still unopened. The second was for those that were now empty. As the night progressed, it was plain to see by the two stacks that the booze was really flowing freely.

Paula and a couple of her girlfriends just weren't getting that buzz that they wanted from the beer. They wanted to P-A-R-T-Y! So, the three went into Paula's bathroom and as Paula turned to shut the door, Kenny came running up. "Wat'cha doing?" Kenny knew what his mother was about to do. He hoped that he could somehow stop her from going ahead. "Mom, can you come here and help me? I can't find the tape with Metallica." "All right Kenny, I'll help you find it.

"Paula said, as she turned back towards the two in the bathroom. "Save some stuff for me. I'll be back in a few." She closed the door behind her as the girls in the bathroom began to giggle.

At least for awhile Kenny wouldn't have to worry about where he would find his mother when she went unconscious. He even begged her for a dance with him in hopes that this would keep her busy...and he hated to dance. Things went pretty good for the next couple of hours. The two that had been snorting in the bathroom were now out cold on the living room floor. One lay there with her legs sprawled across the others lap. Though they both wore dresses, they were not aware of how pitiful they looked with their panties showing.

Paula had begun cleaning up the mess in the kitchen. As she began to fill the sink with hot water, she placed the dirty bowls into the sink that had once help chips and dip. Paula's boyfriend, Juan came in from the living room and dropped a glass into the water. Unfortunately, he was too drunk to realize that he had thrown the glass in the soapy water. "Ouch! Damn it Juan! I'm bleeding!" She grabbed her right hand with the left one. The bubbles from the dish water began to run down her arm, as did the blood. Juan just looked in total shock at what was going on. He was too drunk to figure out how to solve this problem. "You're useless!" She yelled. She quickly passed by the staggering man and helped herself to a towel in the hall cupboard. She knew she didn't have money for going to the hospital. She was going to have to take care of this herself.

Paula made her way toward the bathroom. She opened the medicine cabinet and pulled out the roll of gauze that had sat in that very spot for the past two years. She frantically tore open the wrapper as it dropped to the floor. As she picked it back up, she turned and put down the toilet seat so that she could sit while trying to take care of her wound. She opened the towel and prepared herself to look at the cut. She felt queasy inside. She just hoped she wouldn't pass out when she saw it. As she opened the towel, she was able to see the two inch lesion on the back of her hand. The pain was getting worse. She could really use a snort right now. She finished bandaging her wound as best she could and then went over to place the rest of the gauze back in the cabinet. She was a bit shaky as she reached to place the box up on the third shelf, and it fell back down onto the counter top. Much to Paula's surprise, it dropped next to the line that had been left for her to snort. Just as she had requested. This was too good to be true. Now she would be able to get rid of the pain. She didn't deserve that pain. Within minutes Paula was feeling just fine. She had managed to go back into the living room before finally collapsing on the sofa. She figured she would just stay there for the night. She wanted Juan to apologize. After all...it was his fault she had suffered this accident. It was still dark outside when Paula awoke from a very deep sleep. She realized that she needed to go to the bathroom, and pulled herself up, and slowly staggered her way to the open door. All of the sudden, Juan heard a loud scream coming from the bathroom. As he ran down the hall, he assumed that she was dealing with some problem due to her hand injury. "I'm coming babe!", he yelled as he got closer to the opened bathroom door. "No! Don't come in! Call 9-1-1!" Paula began to cry as she saw before her something that she never realized would be affected by her evening of drugs and booze. There on the floor lay a newborn baby boy. His hands were blue, as were his lips. Paula had been unaware of the fact that she was in labor. She had actually gone into labor because she was using. She had not even really acknowledged the pregnancy. So this took her totally by surprise. She knew that she couldn't help him, and she tried to place him in a towel that hung over the towel rack in front of her, she began apologizing to the baby. " Oh mi hijo. I'm sorry mi hijo!" Little gasps of air could be heard as he struggled to take a true "first breath". Hopefully the medics would get there before it was too late. As she wept at the sight of the child on the floor in front of her, she heard the sirens getting closer. She didn't even attempt to cover herself up as the men worked their way into the bathroom.

"Tom, give me a bulb syringe!" Tom quickly handed his partner the syringe. "I've gotta get this baby out of here, there's not enough room to work here. Give me some scissors and a couple of clamps." His rubber gloved hands worked to clamp off the umbilical cord. The scissors were placed in his hand and he now cut the cord. Though the baby was still gasping for air, he was still blue. No cry had come from his tiny mouth. The medic held the tiny babe in his hand as he stepped over Paula and went out into the dining room. Tom went on into the bathroom to work on Paula. It was obvious to Tom that this woman was high when she delivered. "I'm sorry. I'm sorry." Paula sobbed. I didn't even know he was coming. I didn't feel a thing. Tom waved for the attendants to come over with the gurney. There wasn't anything to be gained by discussing the use of speed while pregnant. All anyone could do now, was to pray. The gurney that carried Paula passed by the area where they were working on the fragile little boy. An officer met Paula at the front door. He followed her to the ambulance, where he informed her he would meet her at the hospital and speak with her further.

As the first ambulance pulled out, the second was arriving in it's place. Inside the little apartment, Tom was busy providing oxygen to the baby. His first cry was a joyous sound to all in the room. "Okay, let's get him into the ambulance. I'll ride in the back with him." The medic carried the tiny one out to the ambulance where he climbed in and sat down in the seat next to the driver. Sirens blared as this precious life was being whisked to a nearby hospital. With time, everyone hoped little Tyler would be all right.

We got a call from Janice at Social Services. She told me that she was in charge of a little boy's case, and his name was Tyler. I asked her to tell me a little bit about him. She said, "Why don't you set up a time to go see him?" I reminded her that I never like to see the babies before I sign up to take them. "Debbe, are you sure you don't want to see this one? I already had one family go out and look at him. They said he didn't do anything for them, so they turned him down." Janice declared. I was completely shocked by her statement and responded with the following question. "What do they mean, he doesn't do anything for them? I thought we were supposed to do something for him." Janice agreed that this is exactly what she thought. "I couldn't believe what I heard. Do they want him to do windows for us or something like that?" We both chuckled and then she again repeated the offer to allow me to visit with the baby before making a decision. I told her to just bring him on over. We could love him and care for him no matter what he looked like.

The following morning, Bejay, Elizabeth and Emily all anxiously peaked out the front curtains hoping to get a glimpse of the newest baby that would temporarily be entering our home. Since we had already adopted three and had two other birth children, Dave made me promise that we would only foster this one and not adopt.

As the white van pulled into our drive way, the children squealed and ran towards the front door. They could barely contain themselves as little 1 month old Tyler slept in the car seat. They all wanted to touch him and hold him. After I finally got Janice and Tyler in the house, I was able to see this precious little baby. He was dressed in a velvet black and white tuxedo sleeper, with a little red bow tie. His dark complexion lead me to believe he was either Indian, Hispanic or Asian. He had beautiful eyes that were gray in color. They were slanted upward at the outside edges. How could anyone think that this child wouldn't do anything for them?

We took Tyler in for a physical within the first few days of his arrival. The doctor looked at Tyler and after considerable contemplation explained to me that he thought this little boy had some brain damage and needed to see a neurologist. I still have the list that the doctor gave me. He high-lighted certain specialists. The other children were in the room with me at the time in the doctor's office. I watched the doctor as he looked at the other three children in the room. These wee children that had all come to see him when they were in a state similar to Tyler's. The doctor turned and looked at me. He smiled and said, "On second thought...just take him home and fix him. You know what to do, just fix him."

I took that little baby home and with love and extra attention, Tyler didn't appear to be the same little baby that he was when I got him.

Update...

Remember that promise that I made to David, not to adopt any more children? Well, I was willing to keep that promise, but David came to me when Tyler was almost six months old and said, "Honey, I really love this little guy, can we adopt him?" Prayer works! Tyler became a Magnusen in 1996. He loves wearing costumes and would wear one to school every day if he had is way. His nick name is Tigger as he is a bouncing bundle of energy. He is very proud of the fact his is our "Tigger". His birth brother, Kenny is back at the institution where he had been four years before. Paula is doing well. She actually went on a talk show to thank me for loving her and adopting and loving her son. She has stopped using drugs and currently works. She stopped by during the holiday season to bring a greeting card to Tyler. He is very proud of this and shared it with many that came over the following weeks.

Don't Forget Our Little Pooh!

My favorite social worker, Janice called in late June of 1994. She knew we had enclosed the far end of our living room in order to make a nursery for another baby or two. She told me about a little boy that was currently in an Emergency Shelter Home and he needed a place that would be willing to take him for at least 12 months. He was only 6 weeks old. She warned me that this little guy was very special. He had a belly button hernia that was "large". I told her that wouldn't be a problem. All I needed to do was contact the foster mother that was currently taking care of him.

Well, the conversation with the foster mother was quick and to the point. I was informed that this little guy was screaming much of each day, and the hernia he had developed since his arrival in this home was pretty overwhelming to look at. I discovered that this little boy was being propped up in a carrier seat in front of a "big screen" television. Supposedly his favorite shows were the news and Big Bird. After hearing these bits of information, I knew that this extra stimuli was horrible for the baby and I had to get right up there and start caring for this sweet little babe.

Within and hour I was looking at the little boy that would consume much of the next week going through withdrawals. My first glance of him was in the carrier, propped in front of the "big screen" television. I was given the outfits that had been purchased for him by the Emergency Shelter mother. I was provided with his medical history and eventually got around to see the front of this little boy. His eyes were huge! I had never seen such big brown eyes on such a little person before. He had no hair to call his own. All in all, I think he bore a close resemblance to the Stay-Puff Marshmallow-Man. I picked him up and placed him in the van where all the other children were anxiously waiting to meet him. Everybody fought for a glance at this little guy. "Where'd those big eyes come from Mommy?" Tyler asked as Emily waved in the baby's direction. Slowly Jonnie turned his head toward the hand that was motioning. Though he didn't return her smile, he did manage to make his eyes even larger while trying to glance toward Emily.

We got everyone safely home and placed Jonnie in a carrier on the dining room table. We wanted to give him a chance to slowly get used to all of us. The reality of what this little boy was about came when he soiled his first diaper. Wow! That wasn't a hernia, it was more like an alien! It stuck out of his belly about 1 1/2 inches, and was the width of a nickel. He was pretty fragile because of all the stimuli that he had been subjected to. The screaming began within a couple of hours. I swaddled him and held him as much as was needed. The most frightening part of this whole thing wasn't the fact that he was going through withdrawals, but the fact that his little belly would push so much fluid into his hernia as he screamed. It would get so big and tight that I was afraid it was going to explode. Finally we were able to get him calmed down. I'll admit, the first few nights were long, but eventually, the hernia began to reduce in size as he began to scream less. Amazing what can happen when a baby avoids the television and extra stimuli.

The next two years were filled with lots of changes. The entire family was in love with this little "toe headed" boy. I remember when it came time to discuss whether or not we wanted to adopt him, Bejay, Elizabeth, Emily and Tyler all sat at the dinner table along with Jonnie and me. Bejay, in all his wisdom said, "Dad, think of this, if Mom hadn't asked you to adopt all of us, you would be sitting at the dinner table by yourself right now." We all voted that night and the entire family wanted to make him a permanent part of our family.

Update...

After being our foster child for a year, I asked the judge for standing in court. This is where you have the right to go to all court proceedings and get a copy of all court documents as well, as give your input to the judge. On several occasions I took Jonnie's mother to court as she had no vehicle. The last time that she went to court was when they were going ahead with a "26" hearing. This is when they take away the parental rights because the parents have not followed the plans that the court had ordered them to do. Instead of standing up and trying to defend herself, she stood up and told the judge that she knew that Jonnie was loved by us and that her wish was that we would be able to adopt him since she couldn't keep him. What a wonderful gift she had given us.

Jonathon Taylor Magnusen became legally ours on January 30, 1998. Before going to court, we told Jonnie that he was going to be adopted that day. He stated to all of us, " I'm the last green Magnusen." After a good laugh we headed off to the court house where my best friend, Julia acted as our attorney. This was a very special moment, and one that took almost 4 years to accomplish. With this, we hung up our foster care hats and looked towards even bigger and brighter things ahead.

107

As the Sun Slowly Sets in the West...

Before this book ends, I want to let you know that even though this can be a very cruel world, there is a lot of love and warmth in it as well, and you will find a large portion of it in the foster families of America.

Thanks to a dear friend, Yvette, I was made aware of the fact that through my opening up about my personal struggles with a heart condition, I might give the readers a deeper understanding of just how deep my passion for the abused, abandoned and neglected children of this world runs.

I'm sure that many of you must figure that in order to take on one or two of the 400,000 to 700,000 babies born each year with drugs flowing through their veins, one must pass some great IQ test or go through basic boot camp. Not so. First and foremost it takes a heart filled with love. Fortunately it doesn't take a heart that only beats 70 beats a minute. If that were the case I could never have gotten into fostering; mine beats as high as 160 beats a minute while sitting still without medication. You see, when I was pregnant with my second "original model" child, Lani, I became very ill. Supposedly you can't get mononucleosis while pregnant but...I did. I also got pneumonia during this time. By the time I was 5 months pregnant I was fighting to stay alive for the sake of my baby and myself.

Every week Gary, from Seal's Healthcare, would drop off a new 5 foot tall drab green tank of oxygen at the foot of the living room sofa. I had a 30 foot long piece of tubing that connected to my mask and then to this tank. I was allowed to get up and "powder my nose" or waddle into the bedroom. The highlight of these visits was when I would get to send a message to one of my old classmate's dads. Her name was Aissa and her dad was "The Duke," or John Wayne. He would get his tank delivered after I got mine and so I would look forward to sending a message to him through Gary. It's funny how a little tiny thing like that could give me a boost of energy.

The prognosis wasn't good. I was placed on two experimental heart medications. No one could tell me what the chances were for both my baby and me. The doctors had told me "You're a walking time-bomb," and "We can't guarantee that you and your baby will survive the whole pregnancy. You could go into cardiac arrest on the delivery table, or your baby could be born blind or retarded." So with plenty of time on my hands to do nothing and lots and lots of time to think, I began to look to the future. I knew that I had no guarantees on a tomorrow and so I wrote my will so that my first born son, Brian would

109

be taken care of in case I didn't make it. I remember telling my husband "I think the babys dead, because I never feel it move." There was no emotion, no panic or even a concern about going to the doctors and getting this checked out. I believe this was "Pregnexia". This is the same feeling that these girls have when going denying their pregnancy.

I decided that laughter had to be a big part of my life. If I was going out, I was going to go out happy. And so, I Love Lucy, Dr. Schuller and MASH became everyday events. Thank God Lucy was on four times a day then.

Since I am writing this and will not claim to be a ghost writer, you can correctly come to the conclusion that I survived the pregnancy. Our daughter Lani is now an adult and she was married the summer of 1997. She is a wonderful, living example of a miracle.

I won't ever take a day for granted. I know that at any point in time my heart could decide to take it's last beat. I learned that no matter what I go through I want to be able to say that I have done the best I can with what God has given me. If I can go to bed each night knowing that I have done my best to better the life or lives of others, then I can sleep peacefully.

With approximately 2.3 million child abuse cases being reported each year, Dave and I decided before we were married that we wanted to keep from complaining about the problem and try and do something to change this BIG, bad world. Even if only one life was helped through our efforts, it would be worth it. My close encounter with death placed an urgency in me to begin fostering sooner than originally expected.

Never in my wildest dreams did I think that I would be opening up doors into my own soul as well as those of friends, family and little short people that came fearfully into my arms for care. For a woman who looked a lot like Mr. Mom when changing a messy diaper on her own two children - (complete with vomiting) - it's been quite a remarkable accomplishment to have now had over 30 babies. I don't want to know how many diapers have passed through my home, but now...I can handle it like a M-O-M.

I hope that if nothing else is learned from this brief adventure into my life and the lives of others, you will be able to see that it doesn't always take a ming vase in order to create a blue ribbon photograph. One can simply use an old tin can and still create a winning masterpiece.

We have learned more about giving than we could ever have learned from a book or a sermon. We have learned that when we give of ourselves in a selfless manner, (even when the assignment seems...well, "yuckky"...) God can, and will work through you, and bless you beyond your own belief. Our Bejay is the perfect example. Remember that funny looking "child of ET and Yoda?" Well, he grew on us, and in us, and we could never imagine life without him.

I have a necklace I call my "lucky charm." It was given to me by my youngest sister a few years ago for Christmas. I really loved that charm, and couldn't wait to buy a necklace so I could wear it. After taking it home and placing it on my dresser, I never saw it again. About a month after the strange disappearance of my new charm, it finally dawned on us that maybe the missing charm and our backed-up toilet were part of the same mystery.

After trying all the usual methods of unstopping it, we ended up taking the toilet completely apart. We had to convince our daughter that there would be a very large sum of money for her if she would be willing to put her small hand up through the bends and curves of the base of the toilet. Off she skipped, happily contemplating what she would purchase with her newfound wealth. When she returned she was wearing my bright yellow Playtex gloves, and a smile glowing with confidence. A short time after starting "surgery," she and her Dad retrieved the small plastic case containing the charm I had been so agitated over losing. If it hadn't been for Bejay and his curiosity, we wouldn't have had the opportunity of rewarding Lani so generously. Darn...too bad my birthday didn't fall that following week. I'm sure my gift from Lani would have been gorgeous - (due to the increase in her income!).

It seems all children at least once come up with some great idea- an idea that in retrospect never fails to bring a smile to their parents' lips... I can remember one very long day, when the three toddlers - Bejay, Emily and Beth - had been extra fussy. They were not the only ones. Their big brother, Brian was also in a "charming" mood. I finally said, "Brian, please go take a nice hot bubble bath." He did a double take, and said, "But I've never had one." At this point, I explained it was about time to have a new experience, so he proceeded to do just that...

I had started a new mission...organize and clear out my daughter's disaster of a bedroom. While Brian was taking his bath, I went back in Lani's room to search for the floor. Below the stacks of paper plates, dirty clothes, and who knows what else was lurking in the shadows- we actually located the carpet. I decided that this was a five-man project, but there was only one woman, one preteen daughter and three fussy, yet energetic babies to do the work.

We brought in two large trash cans and went to work sorting the bad from the good, the junk from the collectibles, and so on. After working for almost an hour, we were able to see we were actually accomplishing something.

At this point in time, I realized I desperately needed to use the restroom. When I entered the bathroom, I stopped dead in my tracks. Before me was the toilet, training potty seat in place, and up through the center of the seat came a mountain of bubbles that flowed over the entire seating area.

Brian's bubble bath had evidently been VERY concentrated. His bubbles had made their way through the pipes, down into the plumbing directly below. All I could do was laugh hysterically, as I looked at the bizarre sight. I kept my legs crossed while I took a Polaroid of this unique experience. I was sure no one would believe just how crazy it looked.

Not everything in foster care is fun and games. There are some serious sides to fostering and I feel that they need to be dealt with too. Just as there is a risk in "sleeping" with more than one bedroom partner, there is a risk involved in caring for children born into these unhappy situations. Our family has chosen to continue to care for these unfortunate ones, regardless. Understanding the risks, we have had the whole family tested for AIDS, as well as taking the usual precautions against all diseases. There is a real need for homes willing to care for the HIV positive children. The only thing I can say is, remember to consider your family when deciding whether or not to care for these children.

Every year, foster parents are required to retake CPR instruction. This particular year, we had our local support group offering the training. The sessions took place at our home, so the little ones watched, as we went through the instructions and actually practiced on the dummies supplied.

Two mornings after our CPR instruction, I was up early with our ESH baby as well as with Emily. I decided to go back to bed, and Emily asked if she could come in with me. I told her that was fine, so we snuggled up under the covers. I was lying on my back, and had just started to drift off to sleep when I felt this short person blowing on my mouth. I asked Emily what she was doing, and she finally was able to help me understand that she was giving me CPR. I guess I had stayed so still, she decided I needed some air. I thanked her for saving my life, then decided to get up for the day.

Before Dave and I began to care for foster children, we had a Cadillac Seville as well as a sports car. Everything revolved around when we wanted to go out to eat, and where we wanted to "play" with Brian and Lani. As you can probably imagine, this has all changed.

We have purchased the largest van that Dodge makes, and learned to live with paper plates more often than the good china. A picnic on the front lawn is much easier than trying to wipe up three or four spills at each meal.

Simple things can be so enjoyable. For example, one day I took Bejay, Beth and Emily to help deliver an order of homemade cream puffs. We had to enter a big, beautiful building definitely meant for adults. The banister was made of rosewood and brass. The entry way was done in imported Italian ceramic tile. My only fear was that they were going to tackle the plants as we went by, or start listening to their voices echoing in the hall. I was lucky, however, and was able to keep them fairly well under control, so long as I promised they could all help run the alligator...I mean, elevator. (You see what hanging around little people who dribble and spit all the time can do to a person?)

After a ten minute discussion of the difference between elevators and alligators, we said good-bye to our friends, and headed back down the "alligator" with Emily pushing the call button outside the elevator, Bejay pushing the floor button inside, and last but not least, Beth pushing the call button again after we got off. Yes, simple-yet very important to them.

I thank God that we have so many wonderful memories that we can hold close to our hearts. We have learned to laugh when many would get frustrated and give up. We have learned to open back doors or windows, if the front door is shut on a challenging situation. We have learned that the house may need dusting, but it can wait a bit longer if a child needs to be held or comforted. There will always be more dust, but when a child is gone, all we have left are memories. We have learned that when somebody-(and I won't mention any names)-gets into my lipstick, I'll get out the camera and take a picture, before that little one helps me scrub the wall.

I guess what I am saying is that Life is too short. Remember to live each day to its fullest, for we have no guarantees of a tomorrow. Some little short person out there could be having the opportunity of his or her lifetime. And you could be the one who teaches them what God's love really is. What could be more gratifying than meeting that child again at Heaven's gate?

What on Earth is Project Cuddle?

Project Cuddle is something that came from my heart. Some say I *am* Project Cuddle. That certainly wouldn't be an insult to me. But, I like to think that somewhere deep inside of all of us there is a bit of Project Cuddle. Here, let me explain. About 10 years ago, I was caring for a foster child that was almost 3 years old. Every time a police car would come in our neighborhood, this poor frightened little girl would run over and grab hold of me. Finally, after seeing this happen at least three times, I decided to ask her why she was hiding. She got tears in her eyes as she said, " I don't want them to take me back to jail."

I explained to the little girl that she hadn't been in jail, the officer had picked her up and taken her someplace that was safe, because she was special.

I decided to find out exactly what had happened to this little girl and see if perhaps it had happened to others. Though the system is put in place for the sake and safety of the children, I discovered that no one had taken the time to remember what it felt like to be a frightened child in a traumatic situation. They were so busy trying to save the child from harm that they didn't realize that a child could actually think of them self as a "bad person". For the children who were being brought into protective custody, that lack of explanation causes problems.

For Candy, it had been very traumatic. She had finally gotten to sleep that hot July night, when she and her little sister were startled by the sounds of a pounding on the front door. Next came the voice of an officer as he yelled for Candy's mother to open the door. Candy had always been fearful of "The Men in Blue", most likely because her mother would often see them drive by and yell "Quick, hide the stuff, the cops!"

Without any warning they watched in horror as their stoned mother was handcuffed and then placed in the back of a patrol unit. She wondered if they would arrest her next. They didn't put her in hand cuffs, but they put her in the back seat of the police car along with her sister, Julie. Next, they were taken to a big building where their clothes were taken off and photos were take of their bruises. After they finished with that horrible task, they put on an outfit that had been provided by a social worker. Their clothes and toys they had carried with them were now placed in a big trash bag. Candy thought that she must have done something really bad to end up with these terrible things happening to her. Julie clung to Candy. Everything was so strange to her. She didn't understand at the age of 18 months what was happening, but she knew it was bad. Finally, after sitting in a lobby for 2 ½ hours, a large woman in a bright flowered dress came over and picked up Julie. Julie screamed in terror, and began to kick the woman. "Now, now, everything will be all right" the woman stated. Nothing was said to Candy. She stood there in total shock. Everything she loved and cared for was gone now. Would she be next to go through those big double doors? Sure enough, within 30 minutes Candy was taken by the hand to a room that housed other children between the ages of 2 and 3. She was shown a little bed that would now be hers until this horrible nightmare stopped. That first night was so scary. She couldn't sleep because of all the other children who were crying for their mothers. She never wanted to see a policeman again. After all, one had brought her to this jail.

After much research, I found out that about 85% of all those children that come into the system are brought in by the police. This meant that there were many that would mistakenly think that they were criminals. When I put myself in these children's shoes, I realized the terror each little child must go through. I realized that if it were me, I would want to hold onto something for dear life. Thus...the name Project Cuddle was born. Since that time we have provided stuffed toys for patrol units all over the country. We have heard wonderful stories of children who have benefited from such a cuddly animal, as well as from officers who found the experience to be a very positive one.

After creating that program we became a non-profit charity. We also managed to expand what our program was about. We decided to let those frightened children who couldn't be with their parents during the holiday season know that they are special. As of January 1998 we have held seven such holiday parties for up to 501 abused, abandoned or drug-exposed children. It's been such a blessing to see their little faces light up and know that at least for a short while they have forgotten the horrible fact that their family isn't able to be with them. The punch flows, the choral groups sing, and Santa and Mrs. Claus grin from ear to ear for each child's photo.

But, Project Cuddle didn't stop there. We found that without even knowing it, we had become pioneers in the care of drug-exposed babies and toddlers. More and more professionals and foster/adoptive parents wanted to know what techniques we were using to care for these babies whom many called "border babies". As many as 22,000 babies a year stay in institutions with no one to love them. It's amazing to me how misunderstood these wonderful children are. They aren't monsters with five heads or 4 noses. They can be wonderful people too. You ask how I can make such a statement. It's simple, Dave and I have adopted 5 such children and they are wonderful. They all love each other, are able to go to public school and follow along with their classmates. We can't imagine our world without them.

We now speak in high schools and colleges, letting young people know that when they use and abuse drugs, they may not be hurting just themselves, but their unborn babies as well. And guys, you are responsible too. They have found that the sperm is affected by something as simple as beer. No baby deserves to be created at a disadvantage just because someone isn't using common sense.

Our speaking engagements have now expanded to include the newest of programs to enter the Project Cuddle gates. We have a nation wide program whose goal is to stop babies from being abandoned in dumpsters or back alleys. In only 18 months, we have saved 51 babies from such a fate. You might wonder how. Well, let me share with you how this exciting program came about.

March of 1996: While reading the local paper, I read "Woman finds newborn crying in a box in front of her home. The infant was the fourth baby abandoned this year in Orange County and the second in less than a week." This one was going to make it. Not all of those found in the county would survive their lonely abandonment. I asked myself the same question so many of us ask ourselves. "Why didn't she bring it here? I would have taken care of it." Then I went ahead and asked the next question that most people never get to. That question is, "How are they supposed to know that we are willing to take that child?"

I tried putting myself into the position of the mothers. Why would someone do something so horrible to an innocent baby? What could she possibly be thinking? I realized that she was probably very frightened of either her family, the authorities or social services. Somehow the key was going to be letting these frightened women know that someone was willing to help them. Perhaps a hot line that girls/women could call in on. If we could ask them to call if they were going to abandon their babies and at least let us know where they had placed the baby, we could go ahead and send someone out to pick up the baby. For the next three months I kept busy putting the program together and getting the volunteers ready to man the phones. During this same time, five more babies were abandoned within Orange and Los Angeles Counties alone. This made me even more determined to get this program off the ground. The one that touched me the most was a little baby girl that had been found locked up in a filing cabinet for almost 2 weeks before someone discovered the body. This pro-

119

gram would be dedicated in memory of her. To me, her name would be Angel.

With training manuals written and volunteers spending time learning how to deal with calls, we were ready to launch the first National toll free crisis line for women that are contemplating abandoning their babies.

July 8, 1996: The big day came and we had news reporters from the local newspapers and our local cable station on hand to cover the story. That evening we got a call from one of the largest Hispanic television stations and they wanted to come down and interview us for the 11 o'clock news. My friend Pilar had to do the interview because I barely spoke Spanish. She knew the subject was serious, but was so nervous that she kept giggling. Eventually she got through it, and felt good with the results. Little did we know how much of an impact this one little segment would have on so many lives.

Before noon the following day, we had received our first crisis call. The woman on the other end of the phone said, "I am about to have a baby. I hate it! If you don't find some place for it, I am dumping it in the park." Boy, did that send all our hearts to pounding. This wasn't what we had planned on at all. What were we going to do?

My husband Dave and Pilar went up to the park where the woman was supposed to be waiting. There she stood by a pay phone where she had probably made the call to our hot-line. She stood there with her little son who wasn't more than 3 years old. He was neatly dressed and held tight to his mother's hand as she, along with her very big belly climbed into the back seat of the Toyota. Poor Dave had no idea what the conversation was about as it was completely in Spanish, but he could tell the woman in the back seat was angry.

The very pregnant woman, (we'll call her Teresa) kept her arm around her quiet little son as she expressed to Pilar her anger. We returned home and I showed her into the living room. Her son immediately became enthralled with our 2 year old son, Jonathon. The two boys couldn't understand each others respective languages but they were able to play together quite well. I guess ethnic diversity doesn't come to a toddler's eyes as being an issue. As the two boys climbed, jumped and snacked, we began to unravel the story of this frightened woman.

We learned that Teresa had become the mother of her first child out of wedlock. She had cared for the child since his birth and had always been the one supporting him both emotionally and physically. He was her life. Nothing was ever going to come between him and her. Teresa was going to make sure of that. The father of the child,

Luis would come and see his son about once a week. Now that the boy was almost 3 years old, he had decided to go to court and fight for custody. He didn't like the fact that Teresa was raising the boy. He was worried that he would turn out to be a sissy if he, the macho papa wasn't in charge of his son.

Teresa explained that she had been raped by a "black man" during the fall of the previous year. She met him at a bar. You see...she loved to dance. She had gone to a bar where she and her girlfriends would gather. They loved to pick up guys and dance. Yes, she may be Mexican, but she was crazy about America's music from the 70's. As she spoke about the music, her eyes lit up. It was as though she temporarily forgot that she was carrying a baby in her swollen belly. Her face got more serious as she remembered where this conversation was leading. She spoke of how she had walked out of the bar with this man at the end of a wonderful evening. She thought that he seemed nice enough. She offered to have him come over to her apartment for a drink. Her ex boyfriend had their son for the weekend, so she was free to just kick back and relax for a change. What ended up happening would change her life forever.

Though Teresa had been extremely busy caring for her son, she was also riddled with frustration as her ex had decided to seriously pursue the custody of Teresa's most cherished possession, Jose. The months after her horrible encounter with the "black man" were plagued with threatening phone calls from her ex., court papers and many tears. She was probably almost four months along when she realized that she couldn't get away from what happened that horrible October night. She knew that she had to come up with a plan, and she only had another month or so to come up with one.

Just before she began to show at the end of her 5th month, she found a room for rent in a neighboring town. It wasn't as nice as her apartment, but no one knew her there. She would be right down the street from a very big park. This park was going to be the drop off place for "the problem" that had been created in October. She rented the room and slowly began moving things over after work each day. She finished relocating everything just before she popped out of her regular clothes. Her son and she would stay inside the 10 by 12 room each day, and she would only go out at night to get groceries or supplies. She quit her job and was totally relying on the child support in order to pay the rent.

She was so afraid that her boyfriend would take away the precious little boy that she held so close to her heart. For the next four months she focused on the Spanish soap operas and absorbed a daily intake of talk shows and Spanish news. If she felt movement, she tried to ignore it. If she was uncomfortable, she became angry at "it". There was no way in this life time she would ever accept this "thing". She hated it!

Finally, on July 7th (the first day of our crisis line was open), she had seen the story about our program on the news. Until now, she had only one option for this baby within her. She had to abandon it in the park. Now there was hope. When I asked her why she had called our toll free crisis line, she said, "Because I realized after hearing about your program that the trash isn't good for the baby." I strained not to show my surprise. A part of me was in shock and a part of me was thrilled because I knew now that my idea was going to work.

By the time we finished our discussion that first night, we weren't sure if she was going to be willing to find some alternative to abandonment or not. We showed her our wicker basket by our front door. There lay a pastel blanket just right for a newborn babe. Okay, this wasn't what we had planned on. We honestly thought that we would get crisis calls about women that had already given birth and were telling us where they had abandoned their babies. This way, at least the baby would have a fighting chance at survival.

If we could work through this crisis , we would have turned this program into something that was even more incredible than I had ever imagined. We were not only saving a baby from abandonment or death, but we were also saving the mother from breaking the law. When this was over, she would be able to walk away with her head held high. No one would have broken the law, and the baby would be safe.

The following morning we received a call from Teresa. She sounded much happier than when we had last spoken with her. She said that she wanted to give the baby a chance. She wanted us to pick her up and she would let us help her in finding families that she would be willing to confidentially help her in privately adopting her baby.

Pilar and I drove up towards the park. But, this time we passed on by it. She had actually given us her address. I felt very good about that. She was actually opening up to us. We would be in her safety zone. As we pulled up, little Jose ran out of the front door and towards our waiting car. He'd been told he was going back to play with Jonnie. Out waddled Teresa. She had a bright little smile on her face. Yes, she was happy with the decision she had made. It was good to know that things were looking up for her. We loaded her things into the trunk of our car and headed for our place.

After arriving back home we contacted Julia Tischler, attorney at law. Believe it or not, she was referred to me by someone I had just gotten a kitten from. After telling Julia about my hair brained scheme, she promptly told me that she would be willing to help this poor woman in making a safe, legal solution to this very big problem. Boy, was I relieved. Over the next couple of days, Julia and I became real friends. In fact, on day #3 of this crisis, Julia called and said, "I have a question for you..." before she had a chance to ask the question I piped in with, "No, I won't marry you." We both needed a laugh at this point. I'll admit it. There was a lot of pressure for us both on this case. We were working with a woman who was a walking time bomb. We were seriously getting a chance at stopping her from doing something that others had only hoped of doing. With my new friend "Jewels" things were going to be great!

We tried our best to keep Teresa calm. We set up an appointment for her to see an obstetrician whom Julia had located. Julia was able to get a "package deal" with the hospital and doctor, so the cost for the adoptive family wasn't going to be very much.

I met Julia for the first time just four days after originally meeting with Teresa. Our dining room table became the setting for this grand meeting. Our little Jonnie and Teresa's little Jose both ran around the table as Julia presented the legal forms to Teresa and the adoptive family whom Teresa had chosen. I was so thrilled to finally meet Jewels. She looked so much like Goldie Hawn and she had the intelligence and grace of Jacqueline Kennedy-Onasis. She carefully read over each paper. By the end of an hour or so, the couple had relaxed and Teresa was able to raise a smile. Yes, this was going to work out well.

I was the lucky one that got to ride shot gun in Jewels gorgeous red Jaguar convertible on the way up to the doctor's. Billy and Sara Banks took Teresa in their car. It was a good chance for them to get to know each other a little better. We waited patiently in the waiting room to hear the information about Sara and Billy's baby-to-be. After careful measuring and questioning the doctor stepped out into the waiting room. The doctor said, "It looks like she could go another week or two at the most. If you want an ultrasound, we can order one on Monday. It's going to cost more, but it's up to you." He knew what her story was and was willing to induce labor if the baby would be delivered safely. The only way to tell was to do an ultrasound and see exactly how far along she was.

As we left, I could tell that Teresa was depressed by the news. She wanted this baby out NOW! I asked her if she would like to sit in the front seat of the Jaguar. Her eyes lit up. "Yes!" she exclaimed. Such a little thing, but it meant so much to her. I was thrilled she could do it. Just before we got into the car, Julia asked Teresa if she was craving anything in particular. She told Teresa that she was hungry and wanted to treat everyone to lunch. Our newly acquired Mexican friend was craving Chinese food. So, we all went down to Golden Garden right near my home. It was a pleasant time for all of us. Sure, there was a language barrier between us all, but we were all there for the same reason...to help a baby have a fighting chance at a good life.

Saturday morning held a few surprises. When I awoke, I was shocked to hear Teresa shouting in Spanish to Pilar. I asked Pilar to translate what the problem was. She told me that if we didn't get the doctor to deliver that baby TODAY, Teresa threatened to deliver it herself. She'd worked in a labor/delivery clinic in Mexico and said, "I know what to do, so you better figure something out! I'm not going to carry this baby any longer!" Pilar knew that this woman was very serious and told me we had better figure something out.

As I put a call into the doctor, Pilar decided to try and get Teresa's mind off her problem by taking her and her son to the market. It didn't work. By the time they got back, Pilar was a nervous wreck. Teresa had been lifting her son up onto her belly in the hope of causing labor to begin. That wasn't all of it...she had been seen actually climbing over a fence in hopes that would make things happen. Pilar was becoming more upset by Teresa's actions and I knew that we had to at least get in touch with her doctor in hopes he could order an ultra sound. This would determine whether or not it would be harmful to induce labor or not.

The doctor told us to go on into the emergency room and have them take a look at her. I truly prayed that if possible, her labor would start when they did the pelvic exam. First they hooked her up to the fetal monitor and at that point and time there was no active labor. The couple who was hoping to rescue and adopt this baby didn't feel they could afford the ultrasound that would be necessary to decide whether or not to induce Teresa. If they could just hold off for a couple of days they would be able to get a friend of theirs to do it for no charge. The weekend rate was over $1,000. This had just happened so fast that they weren't prepared to incur quite this much expense in such a short time.

Sure, they would do what was necessary but they looked at the weekend ultrasound as an extra expense that could be avoided. What they didn't understand was how angry Teresa was. We didn't want to panic them, but we were afraid that this woman would injure herself in order to get this problem disposed of TODAY. My prayers were heard. Though she hadn't been in labor when the day began, she started shortly after her exam. The adopting family had no idea how stressed

What on Earth is Project Cuddle?

Pilar and I were.

Since Julia was home with Teresa's son, I called to let her know what was going on. She told me she would bring Teresa's little son down when Teresa was close to delivering. It had originally been planned that Pilar would come in and take over when Teresa was ready to deliver. It was unfortunate for Pilar that she ended up having to watch Teresa's son as well as my children while I ended up with the joy of coaching this woman through her labor. When I had gone in that day, I knew at least one more sentence than when I arrived. Those words... "No, puedo!" Simply translated it means, I can't! Every time she would yell that during a contraction I would say, "Oh sure, you're fine."

At one point while Teresa was still in labor, I asked her if it would be all right to let the adoptive family in to see her. She said that this would be fine. I felt that it was important for them to see what this woman was going through in order to give them a child. She, on the other hand would have a chance to see that this family respected her for the sacrifice she was making. She would also be able to share in something with them that was priceless.

It was almost midnight when they wheeled Teresa into the delivery room. The adoptive parents and I gowned up and went into the delivery room. I was right next to Teresa's hip, while the adoptive family was at the back of the room. They looked so frightened. It was as though they were going through the delivery themselves for the first time. Teresa was pretty calm about the whole thing, I guess because she had done this once before. But the eyes of those sweet parents to be, Billy and Sara were truly in a state of shock.

It wasn't long after moving to the delivery room that Teresa began to push. We sounded like a cheering team trying to cheer her on. As I saw the babies head crowning, I knew it was only one or two pushes away. As the baby's shoulders cleared I lifted up Teresa's gown in order to keep her from seeing the baby as it was born. This was a request she made, and I wasn't going to let her down. Out popped a beautiful little baby. I quickly blurted out "Don't anyone discuss what has just happened here." I was afraid they would state that it was a boy or girl out loud. I quickly peeked over to see the sex of the baby and then turned to the adoptive family. I pulled down my mask and mouthed to the adoptive family, "It's a girl."

The two of them just stood there in shock. They could barely perceive what had just gone on. I looked back down at Teresa and told her how wonderful she was. After another half minute or so I looked back at Billy and Sara. They were still standing there in shock. I motioned for them to take a picture and then waved for them to follow the baby out of the room.

Soon the cry of the little one could no longer be heard and I now would be able to relax as Teresa was tended to by the doctor. It was almost an hour later when we left the operating room. There was Jewels, right on time with Teresa's little Jose. As tired as Teresa was, her eyes lit up as she looked at her precious son. This was her life. She now knew she had done the right thing. She never broke the law, her son didn't end up in foster care and she didn't end up in jail. She said to me. "For the first time I think I did something that I can be proud of. I feel really good about this, and people respect me."

I let Julia come in and talk with Teresa. I had waited so long to take a peek at that beautiful little baby. Now, I was gong to get my chance. I was so tied up in knots inside. The fact that this really worked was so unbelievable to me. The fact that a beautiful baby had just been born in front of my eyes was just awesome, and the fact that we made both Teresa and the Banks family happy was the best. As I passed in front of the hospital nursery, the entire Banks family was looking in at the incubator at the far end of the room. Cameras were flashing as I entered through the side door. I could feel the tears welling up in my eyes as I got closer to the sleeping little babe. Sara was still in her hospital scrubs and tears were streaming down her cheek bones and onto her mask as she looked down at her new daughter.

As I got close, Sara looked up and said, "I can't believe this, she is a miracle. Thank you, thank you." We both began to cry as we embraced. We had been through so much in such a short time. It felt so good to know that there truly was an answer to this horrible problem...and I had found it!

Update

It has been over a year since this story took place. Sara and Billy couldn't be happier. They love their daughter with all their hearts. Baby #1 is doing great! She is into everything and loves to talk.

Teresa is doing well. She has a good job now and has moved back near her old friends. She still loves to go out dancing on the weekends, but is much more cautious about whom she dates. She calls at least once every couple of months just to say "hi" and see how we are doing.

The Belly Button Baby

It was 2 o'clock in the morning, and the phone was ringing . I was on duty with the hot-line. I picked the phone up anticipating it was a prank call. No such luck...this was the real thing. The voice on the other end of the phone said, "My girlfriend and I saw you on TV a month ago, and...well, we knew we needed to call you. Well, I just helped my friend deliver her baby. I don't know what to do about making the belly button." Now that woke me up rather quickly. I reached over and turned on the lamp that sat on the night stand. I'd never heard this one before. Okay, I had only seconds to come up with a solution. To stall for a moment I decided to ask her a few questions. Hopefully while she was answering I would be able to think of a solution for this predicament. It wasn't long until I figured out what to do. I would contact an emergency room or a labor and delivery nurse and try and find out what we should be doing.

I explained that I would need a number where I could contact her. Once I had her confidence she let me have the number. I explained that I would contact someone that would know what to do and then call her right back. She told me that the mother and baby were doing all right, and in fact the mother was sleeping.

This is when going to a hospital with so many babies comes in handy. You memorize the main hospital number and now when you need it most, it's permanently tattooed in your brain. Within two minutes I had the labor and delivery nurse on the line. She refused to give me any information. I tried to explain to her that we were working with someone that wasn't going to go to an emergency room, or contact a doctor. This was a woman who was going to abandon her baby! She just couldn't share any information because of liabilities. I knew that I was going to have to go another route.

Two more minutes pass and I am finally on the phone with an emergency room nurse. I had to explain what was going on and he too said that this was not something that he could do because of liabilities. I couldn't, just couldn't let this man hang up on me without an answer to my question. It took me a couple more minutes before I got the information that I so desperately needed. Thank God I would now be able to call back with some help.

I picked up the chewing gum wrapper that I had used to write the girls phone number on. I'm glad I only had an eyeliner pencil to write with, because it was thick enough and dark enough for me to see it through my blurred vision. Okay, this wasn't standard : "take a crisis call" office supplies, but it worked. You'd be amazed at some of the things I have written on when in the midst of a crisis.

After I completed giving this girl the instructions over the phone, I realized that this crisis was only beginning. Her friend was now going to have to come up with a solution that was safe and legal while keeping this whole situation confidential. I explained to her the different options that her friend had to choose from. "I'll have her call in the morning. She's sleeping right now." She said. I could only pray that this girl was really going to call back. All I had learned so far was that the birth mother was 26 years old, and already had a little girl that was 4 years old. She didn't tell anyone but her best friend that she was pregnant. The best friend was the one who had called for help, and hopefully she would be able to convince this birth mother to do the right thing.

One of our volunteers, Kalei and I were scheduled to meet with a corporation the following morning and see about getting a corporate donation. We transferred the hot-line to the cell phone and as we headed towards Los Angeles we got the phone call that we had been waiting for. Angie called and told us that she was the one who delivered a little boy the night before. We explained how we could help. She was truly relieved. She set up a time for us to have four different families call her. They were the Johnsons, the Millers, the Jaderholms and the Richards. This was her ticket out of a bad situation and the baby's ticket to survival.

We got a call from Nancy Richards. She and her husband Preston had stared at the clock just waiting to call at the right time. When they made that anxious call, there was no answer from Angie. Their stomachs filled with butterflies. For fear of someone other than Angie hearing any message that was left on the message machine, the chose not to leave any message at all. Now they weren't sure what to do. They called on the cell phone as we were arriving at the meeting. We explained that all we could do was wait for Angie to call.

The meeting started and it wasn't more than five minutes into it when the cell phone rang again. This time it was Angie calling back. Kalei quickly exited the room. While she was gone, others shared across the board table the different bits of information that needed to be discussed. Kalei returned to the room and quickly came over to my side. She covered the mouth piece on the phone and began to whisper into my ear, "Angie left her house. She's at a pay phone because her sister showed up at her apartment." "Okay, get the phone number and we'll have the families call her there." I told Kalei.

We got through the meeting and hadn't heard anything from Angie. We had to start heading back to the house. Perhaps by the time we got there we would know something. As we pulled into the drive-way, we got another call on the cell phone. It was Angie. " I found them! I found them!" she exclaimed. I wasn't sure what she was talking about.

"Angie is that you?" I asked. Once I was sure that it was Angie, I asked her what she was talking about. She explained to me that she had finally talked to the families and was sure that she wanted to work with Nancy and Preston. I was concerned about the baby. I hadn't heard him cry, and if she had left the apartment in a hurry, where did she put the baby. I asked Angie, "Where's the baby?" She replied, "I told my sister that I had to do the laundry, so I grabbed the laundry basket and left." She didn't answer my question. I again asked her the same question, and she again gave me the same reply. I realized we weren't getting anywhere. I finally decided to ask this delicate question in a different way. "Angie, honey, is the baby in the laundry basket?" "Oh, yes, he's there. He's all right." I was very relieved when I heard this. She just hadn't been able to accept this baby and couldn't talk much about any aspect of his being.

I would now have the dubious honor of calling the Richards and letting them know that they were about to be parents. What a shock it was to the Richards. There were a lot of tears shed that day. Nancy had always dreamed of getting married and having children. These dreams were short lived. When Nancy was in her 20's she was told that she would have to have a hysterectomy because of cysts. She trusted the doctors and allowed them to do the surgery. It wasn't until years later that she would find out that the doctor could have simply removed the cysts. She should have been able to have children, but now that this dream was shattered she doubted that she would ever find a man that was willing to marry her. She felt as though she was damaged goods.

Fortunately, Preston and Nancy found each other. He was so in love with her that he didn't care if she could get pregnant or not. They could always adopt. This gave Nancy hope. Now, this dream of holding a precious little baby in her arms that would one day call her mommy, was only an air flight away.

The next two days were crazy! We had to locate an attorney in the state where the baby was located. Once this was done, we had to get all the important information down and faxed to the attorney so that she could get the proper papers written up back there for them to sign. At one point the attorney called to find out what the Richard's new son would be named. Since the Richards were about to take off on a plane, and the attorney needed this information for the papers they would sign upon their arrival, they only had a quick two minutes to come to a decision. They both agreed on Brandon as a first name and for the second name I suggested Preston's middle name. They were sold on it and we now had another challenge taken care of. There was a form that Angie had to sign before Nancy and Preston could get on the plane and fly out to save this baby. We were able to locate a volunteer in a nearby town that was willing to drive over to a "neutral location" and get the faxed form signed by Angie.

It took until the fourth day to get everything in order. Finally the Richards were boarding a plane to pick up their new son. They had two transfers that seemed to take forever. They called me every time they landed. I would keep them abreast of how things were going with Angie and the baby. Though Angie openly shared any information about the baby if asked, she talked so very much about her daughter Katrina. Katrina was three years old and a true joy to her mother. Angie was a good mother. When she became pregnant with Katrina, it was extremely difficult to let her family know. They were strong Baptists and would not want anyone in their Bible study or church group to know that they had failed at parenting. Angie waited until she was almost five months pregnant to tell her parents of her big mistake.

Angie was lucky. Her parents forgave her for this "accident" and helped her through the rest of the pregnancy. Angie felt so guilty for this big mistake, and though she loved her daughter dearly, she knew that this second pregnancy couldn't ever be found out. After all, one mistake is forgivable, but being single and having two pregnancies was not. They never even suspected this second pregnancy. She wore baggy clothes and held books in front of her belly, or stood behind wing back chairs in order to avoid their discovering this secret.

The flights had been so delayed that the hopes of everyone getting together before midnight of that fourth day dissolved. Nancy and Preston were not only exhausted, but feeling like failures for not having arrived on time. Angie was disappointed and felt that this chapter in her life was never going to end. I on the other hand was petrified that some how someone in Angie's family would discover this secret before Preston and Nancy arrived.

Prayer works! The Richards got the last hotel room available in this tiny town. When they awoke the next morning they called over to Angie's house to find out a time that would be feasible to meet. Angie was so excited that she wanted to meet right then. Within half an hour they met at a local park. Angie had been sitting in her car until the Richards emerged from their vehicle. Nancy was first to spot Angie walking towards them with a tiny bundle in her arms and an adorable little toddler clinging to her skirt. Nancy said, "Angie?" Hoping that this was the right young lady. Angie smiled as she confirmed that she was Angie, and within moments Angie handed this precious baby over to his new mother.

It took another week before Nancy and Preston were allowed to leave the state. They went to visit relatives in the mean time. They also got Brandon to the doctors for a physical. They hadn't asked for his measurements because they were afraid the doctor might suspect that the baby had been born at home with no prior medical care. They just didn't want to risk drawing attention to themselves. I suggested that they take a piece of dental floss and measure him from head to toe. When they got back home they could see how long he was by measuring the string. Secondly, I suggested placing him on the scale at the local meat market in town. The days seemed to pass quickly with this couples, new found lack of sleep and their fascination in watching Brandon's every move. This little boy would be all right.

Update

Baby Brandon is doing wonderfully! I am so lucky to have him living only an hour away. He is such a joy to hug when I've had a particularly tough day. His parents have adjusted so beautifully to being parents. Nancy recently told me that she couldn't have given birth to a child and loved him as much as she does Brandon. He is their world.

Angie is doing great! She was so satisfied with the way things turned out that I got a phone call from her on the crisis line about 4 months after Brandon was born asking if she could be a volunteer in her area. She was hoping to help any other girls that might end up in a similar situation. We are so very proud of her.

Our Carolina Belle

Our hot line had been up and running for a couple of months now, and we were already working on our fourth rescue. This baby was being born in the south. I have never been one to look at person's skin color to decide if I would like them or not. In fact, sometimes I haven't even known the nationality of a person until far into a relationship. I think that is a healthy way to be, and I know I am happy that way. Anyway, the most frustrating situation occurred with this case. When the woman originally called, she announced to me that she was 40 years old and just found out she was 8 months pregnant. She thought she had gone through "the change". She already had 2 children at home and there was no way she wanted to let her family know that she was carrying the product of a one night stand in her womb. She was ashamed. She felt so down about getting into this spot. She had been separated from her husband for so many years. There is no way it could be his. No, she remembered the night she met that man. She only knew his first name. She had been swept away by his charm. She had allowed him into her life for only a fleeting moment...a moment when she was feeling vulnerable. This moment would forever change her life. Now, she was paying dearly.

As I began to contact families that might be willing to rescue this baby, I began by calling those that were nearest to this woman's location.(we'll call her April) There was one couple that already had a couple of children and they were hoping to add another to their family. I thought this would have been the perfect addition. You see, both the mother and father were African America. They lived within 40 minutes of this woman. Not too close, yet close enough to help and rescue. Unfortunately I was wrong. They turned the baby down because the child wasn't part Caucasian. Evidently the father had some Caucasian in his blood line and for this reason they turned this precious baby down. I couldn't understand it. I guess this was because I had cared for and loved children from every color of the rainbow. All I could do was tell myself, "That's too bad, they are the ones that are going to miss out on a wonderful, wonderful little baby."

Because we had only been up and running for a month, we were running out of leads for families. I had even called the local, private adoption agency in that area and they told me they would only work with an African American baby if we provided the family that was going to privately adopt. They just didn't have families willing to adopt African American children. This was so frustrating!

Finally, I found a couple of families that were willing to speak with this frightened woman and hopefully she would feel comfortable with at least one. The one couple was very sweet. They hadn't been married even five years yet, but they were hoping to adopt before they had their own. Then there was a single woman. She was a very gentle woman that had suffered through the loss of twins a few years before. She longed to hold a baby in her arms and was financially very capable of caring for a child. After the twins had died, she had to have a hysterectomy, and so the only way she would ever be able to be a mother was through adoption. I called and asked her if she would consider rescuing this baby. She immediately said, "Yes, I think I could handle it even if there was something wrong with it. I know the risk of downs increases when a mother is older, but it would be loved here no matter what."

April had narrowed things down to two families, the Sampson's and Wendy Jacobs. Wednesday evening was when she was going to call us with her decision. She had told me the day before, I'll talk to all of them, and then I'll pray about it." That night I checked in with April and found out that she still hadn't made a decision. I held back the secret that Wendy's friends had given her a surprise baby shower a couple of days previously. I didn't want it to sway her decision. I decided that if she did choose Wendy I would then tell her about the kindness of Wendy's friends and the new neighbors her baby would have. I called the Sampson family and Wendy to let them know that we would still be waiting. Wendy had been especially good at letting me know where she was when she wasn't at home. The Sampson's were always reachable by pager.

I got the call from April that everyone had been waiting for. She had made a decision. She had chosen Wendy to be the mother of her child. She felt that Wendy would be willing to love this baby whether or not it was born with arms or without. She could handle and love it even if it was a downs baby. April wanted that security for her baby. No dumpster for this baby! Thank God we had gotten to her. Now, I would have to call Wendy and let her know that she needed to get an attorney as soon as possible and get things in motion. I had been given her schedule of where I could find her for the past two days, but now I hadn't been told where she was this day. I called her mother, and she had no idea where her daughter could be. I called all the numbers that I had and yet no one knew where she was. I left messages on her machine, I left messages with her mother. I was beginning to panic. Something had to be wrong. This wasn't like Wendy. She was so anxious to find out if she was going to be a mother. Something must have happened to her. For the next couple of days I would try every number at least four times a day. Her mother still hadn't heard from her.

I was running out of time. April was due in the next week. If I didn't hear from Wendy by noon on Sunday, I was going to have to contact April and let her know that the mother she had chosen was missing. We would have to speak with the Sampson Family or talk to more families. I truly didn't want this, but I knew what would happen if April delivered and no one was there to pick up that baby. I couldn't let that happen. I prayed so very hard, because I knew in my heart that this was a match made in Heaven. I knew that with only a few hours until the deadline, prayer was the only way we would get Wendy to make that call if she was able to. Finally, at 10:00a.m. on Sunday morning I got the call I had been waiting for. "Hi Debbe, it's Wendy. I just got in. I was stranded in the mountains for the past three days." I told Wendy that she had been chosen. She was thrilled and I was relieved.

Finally I could relax because Wendy had such a willingness to accept this precious gift, and I could take a moment and sit back and learn where Wendy had been. She had been cleaning an exclusive hunting lodge high in the mountains. This is a place where corporate executives have to be flown in. There was plenty of food on hand, but not one phone, not even a CB radio. This was a job Wendy did once a year, and with the thought that a baby might be on the way, she wanted to get it out of the way before the baby's arrival. I now learned that the plane that had flown Wendy up there wouldn't start when she was ready to go back home. I had called Wendy's mother, and repeatedly bugged her until she finally realized something must be wrong. She finally called the police with the hope that they knew where she was. Eventually, they sent someone up to find both Wendy and the pilot on top of the mountain. What an exciting week this had been.

Monday morning Wendy got her paper work started. She met with a social worker and we now had to hope and pray that everything would be in order before the baby was born, so she could get there right away. Thursday morning at 4:00 am I received a call from April. She was now in a hospital bed and was in labor. Actually, she was standing on the bed and in labor she told me. So, I quickly called Wendy and told her she was about to be a mother so she had better get ready. By midnight that evening she was on her way to meet the baby of her dreams. She had left the house shortly after I informed her that April was in labor. She had much to do before she took the midnight flight, and there was no way to get in touch with her to let her know that she had a little daughter. April also told me that the baby had clubbed feet. She and I both felt certain that Wendy would still want the baby, but we would have to wait until she got there to let her know about the situation.

Wendy landed back east at 10:00 a.m. on Friday. She had no idea how she was going to get to the hospital, so she went up to a police officer that was standing nearby for directions. As Wendy stood there with a look of panic on her face and a car seat in her hands the officer told her to hold on a moment. The officer went over and spoke to a driver of a hotel courtesy van. She wasn't sure what he was doing. She thought that perhaps that he knew the driver and was going over to greet him. The officer came back in a couple of minutes and had a very large smile on his face. He told her that the courtesy van was about to leave and that they were willing to give her a ride to the hospital as it was directly across the street from the hotel.

When Wendy got in the van she was greeted by a very kind, southern gentleman. As the only hotel passenger in the van, he insisted on allowing her to be dropped off first. She quickly got off the van and rushed towards the hospital entrance. She stopped at the front desk to find out what room April was in. She wasn't positive, but she was pretty sure that she would already have delivered. According to the registration desk there was no one by April's name registered.

I got a phone call from Wendy and she was in tears. She started crying and said, "If she doesn't want me to have the baby then I'll just get on the plane and come back." I calmed her down and told her that I had heard from April and that she was doing well and that she still wanted Wendy to be this baby's mother. I told her to stay by the pay phone and I would call back there as soon as I found April. Finally, I got a phone call from April. She was wondering where Wendy was. I explained that she had been searching the hospital for her because she couldn't find her name at the registration desk. "Oh, I did that so my family wouldn't be able to find me." April had the attorney and her assistant there in her room. I suggested that they go out and look for Wendy at the pay phone.

Within an hour April's attorney and Wendy all found each other. The attorney made a comment to Wendy that upset her. He explained that the baby had clubbed feet and she would need surgery. Then he stated, "You do realize that this is a black baby and you are white, don't you? I mean, this baby already has two strikes against it. She's black and she has clubbed feet." Wendy didn't care. She was willing to take this baby no matter what.

The attorney went back and asked for April to sign the same documents. It was almost time for Wendy's plane to be boarding and she still hadn't met this new member of her family. With only fifteen minutes until she needed to climb back on the courtesy van, she finally saw her new little daughter. As she leaned over to pick up the five pound bundle, she said, "Hi sweet heart, I'm your new mommy." As she spoke, little Angel turned to look at her new mother. This was a match made in Heaven.

Update
The two flew safely back to California when Angel was only one day old. Her middle name became Grace. She now lives in a wonderful community that has embraced her as their own. She has a pot belly pig, miniature horses that are part of her everyday life. This little girl has a chance at a life that most only dream of. At the ripe old age of six months, I finally got to meet this beautiful little girl. I love her dearly. Though I wasn't there for the birth, though I didn't know what she looked like until recently, I have a very soft spot for her in the corner of my heart. Since Angel's birth, she has had two surgeries and is now going through physical therapy. She will soon be walking. She now has a little brother that has been added to her family through our program. I am so proud to know both her and her mother, and look forward to someday meeting the newest member of their family.

The Future of PROJECT CUDDLE

As of February 20, 1998 we have saved 51 babies in only 18 months. This number will increase as we get our number out to those that need to have it. We have learned so much about what these women are like. Over 50% have other children and can be considered good parents to those they have. Over 50% are students or work. We have been able to help many of these women/teens in telling their families. Ultimately many have chosen to keep their babies after we got them past this initial hump. The other interesting fact that we have found is that the average age is approximately 24 ½ years old. Most are hiding pregnancies from their parents, abusive husbands or are afraid of social services taking their other children away as well as this one.

Our goal is to get the word out to those frightened women across the country. We need to let them know that there is help out there for them. All they need to do is call 1-888-628-3353 or 1-88-TO-CUDDLE. They are no longer alone.

FOOTNOTES

1   Janine Anderson, "Drug Babies," Orange County Register, Sept.17,1989, p. 1

2   Suzanne Silverman, "Combinations of Drugs Taken by Pregnant Women Add to Problems in Determining Fetal Damage," JAMA, March 24-31, 1989, p. 1694

3   Highlights of Official Child Neglect and Abuse Reporting 1986, The American Humane Association, (Denver,CO.,1988) p. 23 and 27

4   Highlights, op. cit. p. 23

5   Ken Magid, M.D. and Carole A. McKelvey, High Risk Children Without a Conscience, (Lakewood, CO, CDR Distributors, 1988), p. 183

6   ibid.

7   Ira J. Chasnoff, M.D. "Perinatal Effects of Cocaine," Contemporary OB/GYN, May, 1987, p. 1693

BIBLIOGRAPHY

American Humane Association. Highlights of Official Child Neglect and Abuse Reporting. Denver, CO, 1988.

Anderson, Janine, "Drug Babies," Orange County Register, 17 Sept., 1989, p. 1.

Chasnoff, Ira, J., M.D. "Drug Use In Pregnancy: Epidemiology and Clinical Impact." NAPARE, Chicago, Aug., 1990, pp. 213-17.

Chasnoff, Ira J., M.D. Jane W. Schneider, M.S., P.T., and Don R. Griffith, Ph.D. "Infants exposed to cocaine in utero: Implications for developmental assessment and intervention." Infants and Young Children, July 1989, pp. 26-29.

Chasnoff, Ira J., M.D. "Perinatal effects of cocaine." Contemporary OB/GYN, May, 1987.

Chasnoff, Ira J., M.D. "Special Currents-Cocaine babies." Ross Laboratories. Contemporary OB/GYN, March, 1989, pp. 178-87.

Chasnoff, Ira J., M.D., Don R. Griffith, Ph.D., Scott MacGregor, D.O., Kathryn Dirkes, BME, and Kayreen A. Burns, Ph.D. "Temporal Patterns of Cocaine Use in Pregnancy," Journal of American Medical Association, March 24-31, 1989, pp. 218-21.

Cline, F. Understanding and Treating the Severely Disturbed Child. Evergreen Consultants in Human Behavior, Evergreen, CO, 1979.

County Welfare and Mental Health Directors Associaton. "Ten Reasons to Invest In the Families of California." California State Dept. of Mental Health, 1989.

Falhberg, V. Attachment and Separation: Putting the Pieces Together. Michigan Department of Social Services, DSS Publication #429, 1979.

Greenspan, Stanley I. Parent-Child Bonding—The Development of Infancy. National Committee for Prevention of Child Abuse, Chicago, 1988.

Hare, R.E. "Twenty Years of Experience With the Cheekley Psychopath," Unmasking the Psychopath. W.W. Norton, New York, 1986, pp. 3-27.

Lachnit, Carroll. "Drug-exposed Infants Add Pressure to Hospitals." Orange County Register, Nov. 6, 1988.

Lamb, Michael. "Parent-Infant Interaction, Attachment and Socioemotional Development in Infancy." The Development of Attachment and Affiliative Systems. Plenum Press, New York, 1982.

Magid, Dr. Ken and Carole A. McKelvey. High Risk: Children Without A Conscience. CDR Distributors, Lakewood, CO 80228, 1988.

Oro, Amy S., B.S. and Suzanne D. Dixon, M.E. "Perinatal Cocaine and Methamphetamine Exposure: Maternal and Neonatal Correlates." Journal of Pediatrics, Oct. 1987, p. 57.

Paulsen, Marie Kanne, Ph.D. "Risk Factors in Drug-Exposed Infants and Toddlers." Children's Hospital of L.A.

Ronkin, Sheila, M.D., Jack FitsSimmons, M.D., Ronald Wapner, M.D. and Loretta Finnegan, M.D. "Protecting mother and fetus from narcotic abuse." Contemporary OB/GYN, March, 1988, pp. 178-87.

Ruley, Daniel A. "Compelled Medical Treatment of Pregnant Women." Journal of the American Medical Association, March 24-31, 1989, p. 1730.

Silverman, Suzanne "Combinations of Drugs Taken By Pregnant Women Add to Problems in Determining Fetal Damage." Journal of the American Medical Association, March 24-31, 1989, p. 1694.

Silverman, Suzanne "Interaction of Drug-Abusing Mother, Fetus, Types of Drugs Examined in Numerous Studies." Journal of the American Medical Association, March 24-31, 1989.

Wyngaarden, James B., M.D. "Habitual Fetal Loss May Indicate Autoimmune Disease." JAMA, March 24-31, 1989, p. 1697.

Zylke, Jody W., M.D. "Maternal, Child Health Needs Noted by Two Major National Study Groups," JAMA, March 24-31, 1989.

PHOTO CREDITS